Who Am I?

**BUILDING BLOCKS FOR BECOMING
YOUR BEST FUTURE SELF**

Who Am I?

BUILDING BLOCKS FOR BECOMING
YOUR BEST FUTURE SELF

jenny oyston

Who Am I?
First published in Great Britain in 2023 by
LOTUS BOOKS
An imprint of PARTNERSHIP PUBLISHING

Written by Jenny Oyston
Copyright © Jenny Oyston 2023

A CIP catalogue record for this book is available from the British Library.
ISBN 978-1-915200-27-3

Book cover design by: Partnership Publishing
Book Cover Image ©Shutterstock 200018552

Book typeset by:
PARTNERSHIP PUBLISHING
North Lincolnshire, United Kingdom

www.partnershippublishing.co.uk
Printed in England

Partnership Publishing is committed to a sustainable future for our business, our readers, and our planet; an organisation dedicated to promoting responsible management of forest resources. This book is made from paper certified by the Forestry Stewardship Council (FSC) an organisation dedicated to promoting responsible management of forest resources.

We operate a distinctive and ethical publishing philosophy in all areas of our business, from our global network of Authors to production and worldwide distribution.

Who Am I?
E-Book Available

www.lotusbooks.com

Contents

Part Two - Who Do I Want To Be?

Part Three - How Do I Get There?

Introduction

Hello, and welcome to a book that I hope will help you to see how to improve your mental wellbeing and begin to live a life in which you feel happier and more fulfilled. Whether you are simply feeling curious about what this might mean, or you have been feeling a bit flat and directionless, or if you simply want to be the best you can be, you should find some inspiration here.

I'm not going to talk about serious mental health problems, which benefit best from talking therapy with an understanding counsellor or psychotherapist, and perhaps medication if you and doctor decide this is the right course for you. What we will explore here is how you can take greater responsibility for your own life, by examining what makes you tick, why you behave the way you do (and whether there may be different ways of behaving that would be more helpful) and what motivates you. We'll take time to look at how your emotions affect your behaviour and clarify some of the thinking patterns you have developed and challenge the unhelpful ones. Ultimately, I hope this will encourage you to think about how to develop your potential and become more like the person you want to be!

The ideas you'll find here are just a starting point, and once you start putting some of the suggestions into practice, you'll probably realise that this is something you may continue to do for the rest of your life. As your self-knowledge grows, you will gain a greater sense of control over what happens to you and how you react. However, I'm not pretending that bad things won't happen! Life is full of ups and downs and one thing we'll also think about is how to learn to accept the stuff you can't do anything about.

I hope you find this useful. If you enjoy this book, you may like to go on to read more about mental and emotional wellbeing and discover how so many of the beneficial changes you would like to make lie in your own hands.

Who Am I?

~ PART ONE ~

Section 1

BEGIN AT THE BEGINNING

FIND OUT MORE ABOUT YOURSELF

There are many aspects that contribute towards you being the person you are. This diagram shows some of them and you may have ideas of your own. We are going to explore each of the areas below in more detail as we go on, but you might like to think now about what you currently know about yourself in respect of each of the aspects in the boxes.

Who Am I?

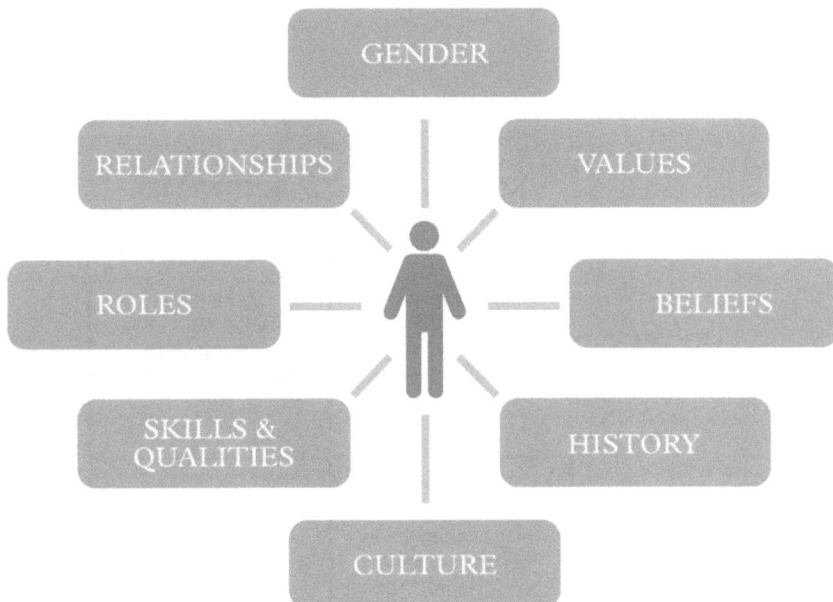

KNOWN AND UNKNOWN – THE JOHARI WINDOW

Achieving genuine self-knowledge requires a much deeper level of understanding. The diagram below, known as the Johari Window[1], is a reminder that our own perceptions may not always be accurate or complete. It summarises different aspects of self-perception and the perception of us by others. We all have these different parts to ourselves.

Part 1 is open to everyone and can be extended by self-disclosure.

Part 2 is a private part of ourselves, containing secrets, shame, guilt etc. We can choose not to share it except in close relationships.

Part 3 is the area we can't see ourselves, but we could learn more about it through feedback from others.

Part 4 is closed to everyone and includes unconscious needs, impulses and anxieties – but also, our untapped potential. Counselling may help us to access this.

	KNOWN TO OTHERS	NOT KNOWN TO OTHERS
KNOWN TO SELF	**1** Known Self Things we know about ourselves and others know about us	**2** Hidden Self Things we know about ourselves that others do not know
NOT KNOWN TO SELF	**3** Blind Self Things others know about us that we do not	**4** Unknown Self Things that neither we nor others know about us

Before going any further, let's think about what we actually mean by the word 'self.' At this stage, it's quite helpful to make a distinction between different definitions which you may come across in reading about self- development:

1.   **Self-image/self-concept**: this is your idea of how you are as a person, including physical, behavioural, and psychological characteristics and aspects of identity. It may include, for example, ethnicity, status, roles and aspects of personality etc.

2.   **Real self**: this is the authentic person who underlies a lot of what we see on the surface; it includes your feelings, both negative and positive. Many parts of your real self lie within the unconscious part of your experience. They include your motivations, your fears etc, whose influence you may not be aware of and may be reluctant to acknowledge. Sometimes, we disguise our real self and develop a 'false self' to deal with difficult situations.

3.   **Ideal self/Self-actualisation**: Many writers talk in terms of moving towards self-actualisation, which could be summarised as achieving full potential, growth, and self-fulfilment. This is a very individual concept, but for example, a person who behaves in a 'real' way can articulate honestly and openly how they feel, what they think etc., without fearing the reactions of others. As you move towards becoming more like your ideal self, you behave with integrity, endeavouring to live your life in the best way you can according to your beliefs and values. Developing true authenticity is a lifetime's work!

None of these aspects of the self is static, but each is constantly evolving and developing.

Who Am I Now?

Depending on your current age and stage in life, the things you focus on, and the priorities you have, will obviously vary. For example, adolescents are very concerned with developing their self-identity; this sometimes involves rebelling against the ideas and values they have been brought up with. Young adults' lives tend to revolve around developing their careers or forming and nurturing a family of their own. Mature adults may continue to be ambitious but may also reach a stage in their work life where they feel they have peaked; maybe they even have a mid-life crisis, where they re-assess their achievements so far and become anxious about how their future will look. Parents can suffer from empty-nest syndrome as their offspring branch out on their own. Those confronting older age may develop new anxieties. Such complex adjustments throughout life will have a profound influence on your mental wellbeing.

Let's now look at some of the features in the diagram on page 1 in more detail. This is where you can start to learn about yourself in more depth. Starting with an easy one first, let's explore the **roles** you currently have in your life. The diagram on the following page gives you some ideas, but I suggest you draw one like it of your own and include any roles which are significant for you.

ROLES YOU PLAY

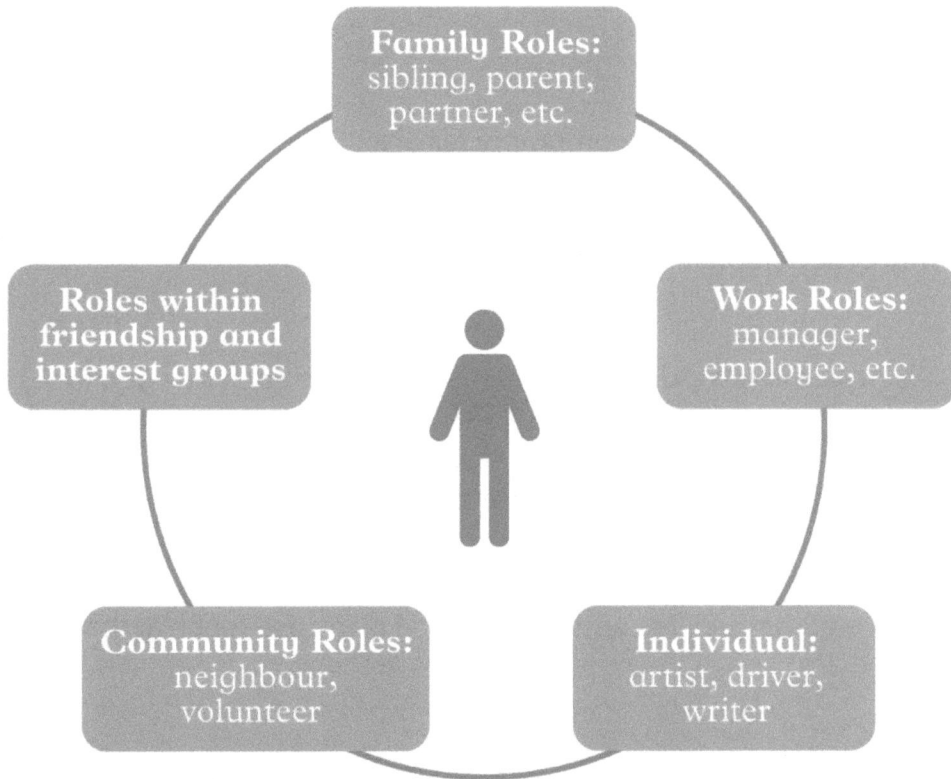

Family Roles: sibling, parent, partner, etc.

Roles within friendship and interest groups

Work Roles: manager, employee, etc.

Community Roles: neighbour, volunteer

Individual: artist, driver, writer

When you look at the roles you play in your life, you may find it easy to move on to considering the individual **qualities** you bring to each.

Try the following exercise to identify some of your strengths and qualities.

When I think about myself in each/any of these roles, I can see that:

- My top 5 strengths are:

- My most useful skills/competencies are:

- My best personal characteristics include:

- Each role is rewarding for me because: (take each one at a time)

- The role I would most like to develop is:

- I have other qualities and skills which I don't use much at the moment; these are:

This will show which personal qualities you tend to attach most importance to and may suggest other things you could develop. Also ask yourself – have you been unrealistically modest/arrogant, or have you been accurate and honest?

Do you think there is a good balance between all these roles in your life? Is there anything you'd like to change?

From here, there is a natural link to **relationships**. How we make and develop relationships is enough for a book in itself! Here, we'll confine our exploration to considering how you are in relationships and how you feel about this.

RELATIONSHIPS IN YOUR LIFE

A place to start is by looking at the relationships you have in your life and how important they are to you. Try to be honest about this and try to stay in the here-and-now rather than referring to things that have happened in the past. Instead of just listing your relationships, think about how important they are to you, by placing them within concentric circles, with the closest in the middle.

Here is an example:

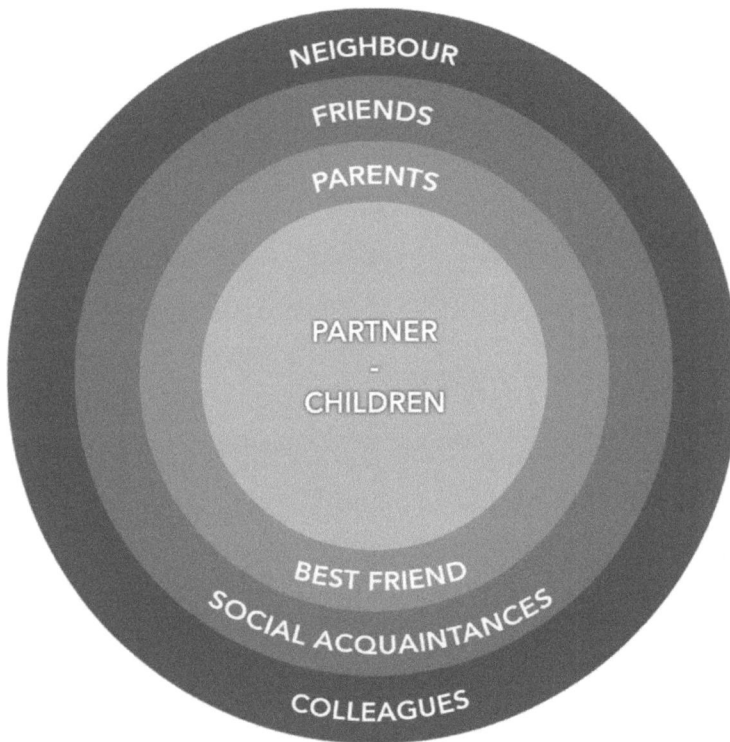

Put in as many people as you like. Where do you think you'd be in other people's circles? Is there anything you'd like to change? Do you think these people know how important they are to you?

Section 2

EXPLORING VALUES

Our frame of reference is our way of seeing the world; it includes the standards and values we have, the beliefs that are important to us, and the prejudices we hold. These have often been part of us since early childhood and are deeply ingrained. However, it is worth examining all these, especially values, and thinking about what really matters to you. Almost everything you do is underpinned by the values and beliefs you hold. Your actions and choices are based on what you believe to be right, just, appropriate, and so on.

As a starting point, think about a decision you made today. At the time, you probably had choices (*Do I let the children find their own way to school or do I take them? Do I arrive at work on time or will I be late? Do I buy a treat for tonight's supper?* etc). Now think about what made you select the option you did. This will begin to give an insight into your values and beliefs. For example, one value may be that you want to be a 'good' parent. You have your own idea of what this means, and you believe you must behave in certain ways in order to achieve it. On the basis of these values and beliefs, you make choices e.g., about whether to supervise your children or help them become more independent.

To clarify and articulate your own values, you might like to try any, or all, of the following exercises:

VALUES 1

Make a list of the qualities or characteristics which you like in other people, and which you hope to demonstrate in your own behaviour. There are lots of examples of such lists, but you might find the following a helpful starting-point:

Acceptance/ tolerance	Flexibility/ Adaptability	Adventurousness
Creativity	Cooperativeness	Belief in freedom and choice
Assertiveness	Courage	Friendliness
Authenticity/ Genuineness	Being forgiving	Appreciating beauty
Fostering curiosity	Being fun-loving	Being caring
Showing generosity	Challenging	Belief in equality
Able to express gratitude	Capable of compassion	Being honest
Showing fairness	Being non-judgemental	Enjoying humour

Making a Contribution	Behaving with humility/modesty	Being hard-working
Being patient	Being Independent	Demonstrating persistence/resilience
Able to be intimate/share vulnerability	Able to take/accept responsibility	Being encouraging/supportive

VALUES 2

Define what for you represents leading a 'good' life. How might we see you behaving in accordance with what you believe to be right? (Your moral values). You might consider here, ideas about fairness/respect or justice in the way you behave towards other people and expect to be treated. For example, in what ways does your behaviour show that:

- You believe that you are entitled to certain things, such as pleasure, freedom etc.?
- You have certain ideas about what 'duty' is?
- You attach importance to taking on particular responsibilities?
- You endeavour to be authentic/real/genuine?

VALUES 3

You may not have explored them explicitly, but you will have ideas about what makes someone a 'good' person. This will have a huge influence on the relationships you have with others, even if you don't realise it. This exercise is designed to help you articulate some of these views. Your behaviour is likely to be affected by your beliefs and ideas, and sometimes you will meet people who don't share them. Will you be able to respect other points-of-view? Try answering the following:

1. Do you (or have you) belong/ed to any groups where moral principles or rules are quite strong (this may be a religious or political group or even your family background)? Such groups have ideas and beliefs about what is right/wrong. List as many beliefs as you can for the groups you have belonged to. Think about the impact of these on you at different times in your life. For instance, have you experienced any tension, doubt, or conflict?

2. Do you have any favourite sayings or proverbs which have a moral dimension to them, such as *'you get what you deserve,' 'forgive and forget'* etc? For each, explain where this may have come from. Do you still believe it now?

3. Consider whether there is any behaviour you feel you simply can't tolerate. How would you respond if you were to see something unacceptable taking place (e.g., someone being bullied or abused)?

This can be trickier than you realise:

I once did an exercise like this and found that three characteristics I value most are *honesty*, *humour,* and *kindness*. However, living a life according to these and other beliefs and principles is harder said than done! For example, if honesty is a priority, does this mean you would *never* lie? If humour matters, might your laughter ever cause distress to someone else? How much kindness are you prepared to extend to others before you feel you might have exhausted your resources, or you might be taken advantage of? Take time to reflect on whether your expectations of yourself and others are realistic.

We also need to respect other people's frame of reference: if you have children, especially as they become older, you might like to consider the extent to which you try to make them into the person you think they should be, rather than learning about and accepting the person they actually are. Similarly, if we are with people who don't think the same way we do, should we try to suspend our judgement in order to listen, empathise with and try to understand them? People who behave 'badly' often have reasons for doing so!

PREJUDICES

In my very first teaching job, each member of staff had to have an excruciating lunch with the Head every week. I used to dread this, and always felt on edge in case I did or said something wrong. For weeks I felt inferior, patronised, and anxious. Then one day, when we had sat down, she said to me, 'I've just realised who you are…' She had learned that my grandfather had been head of one of the most highly regarded schools in the area and was greatly admired. Guess what? From then on, she began to treat me with much more interest and respect. But this wasn't about me! This came from her prejudices around status, achievement and who was worthy of her respect.

Pete Sanders (see bibliography) offers the following definition of prejudice as:

'…an attitude that predisposes a person to think, feel, perceive and act in favourable or unfavourable ways towards a group or its individual members'.

Very often, stereotyping evolves from our perceived views about members of groups, so that individuals are treated as typically having certain attributes, which then lead (with reinforcement from the media) to positive or negative prejudices towards them. By monitoring your reactions to another person, you may become aware of personal barriers or issues that might prevent the development of a helpful relationship. You may identify fears you have about particular groups, or about your lack of experience with someone whose background is very different from your own. Some forms of discrimination can be subtle, and it helps to ask yourself, for instance, whether there are any hidden agendas or implications behind your behaviour towards others.

How aware are you of your own **cultural bias and values**? Do you recognise any (albeit unintentional) social inequality and discrimination? Find some answers to the following questions and you may begin to become more aware of your own (often unconscious) biases:

1. Am I more comfortable in the company of people who are 'like' me?
2. Sitting among strangers, e.g.: on public transport, what features about them do I tend to focus on?
3. What labels do I attach to myself and to people I know? (See the *labels game* on page 17.)
4. What aspects of life do I have strong opinions about (such as religion, politics, education, crime, sexual orientation, unemployment, housing)?
5. Do I think all people have equal rights? This might be examined for instance within the realms of education, work, or state support; you might find you views are different if they refer to different groups of people (e.g.: those of different ages)

Test your biases: Be honest, how would you react if:

*   Somebody 'scruffy' with strong body odour sits next to you at the doctors.
*   Someone speaks with a strong regional accent.
*   A stranger of the opposite sex describes you as 'attractive.' Would this be the same if the speaker was old/gay?
*   A beggar accosts you in the street.
*   You find it hard to understand what a person from another country is saying.
*   You meet someone wearing clothing (uniform/football strip etc) that could be considered opposed to a group you belong to.
*   In a supermarket, a child is having a tantrum and the parent appears to be unable to cope; what are you thinking?
*   Someone with learning difficulties is taking a long time to express what they want to say.
*   You are driving behind someone who appears to be driving very slowly or erratically.
*   A political speaker expresses views that are different to your own.
*   You are in a part of town where the houses appear badly kept and there is lots of graffiti, rubbish in gardens etc.

Over the next few days, try to notice how you react to other people around you and think about what this tells you about your prejudices. The next section has another exercise to explore your prejudices.

LABELS

Perhaps on public transport, or in a café, look around at the people near you and see how much you think you can tell about them just by looking. Obviously, this works best if you don't already know them. Choose labels (you could use those below or make up some of your own) which you think would apply to them. Think of positive as well as negative ones. (It doesn't matter whether you're actually right or not – the point is to learn something about how *you* label people.)

Someone who reads The Sun	Someone who loves children	Someone who plays a sport	Someone who is fond of animals	Someone who thinks appearance is very important
Someone who likes to help others	Someone who likes to be different	Someone who eats lots of sweets	Someone who has travelled a lot	Someone who has had a hard life
Someone who has a strong temper	Someone who has plenty of money	Someone who has a great sense of humour	Someone who reads a lot of 'serious' books	Someone who doesn't like loud noise
Someone who didn't do very well at school	Someone who gets bored easily	Someone who is happy with who they are	Someone who doesn't have much respect for authority	Someone who isn't very confident

Now think about how you label yourself! This is just one step towards getting to know yourself. It involves thinking about (often unconscious) messages you give the world and yourself; if you label yourself in a certain way, chances are, you live up to these labels! Look at the examples given below and see if any of them fit the labels you wear. Are there any others that you give yourself?

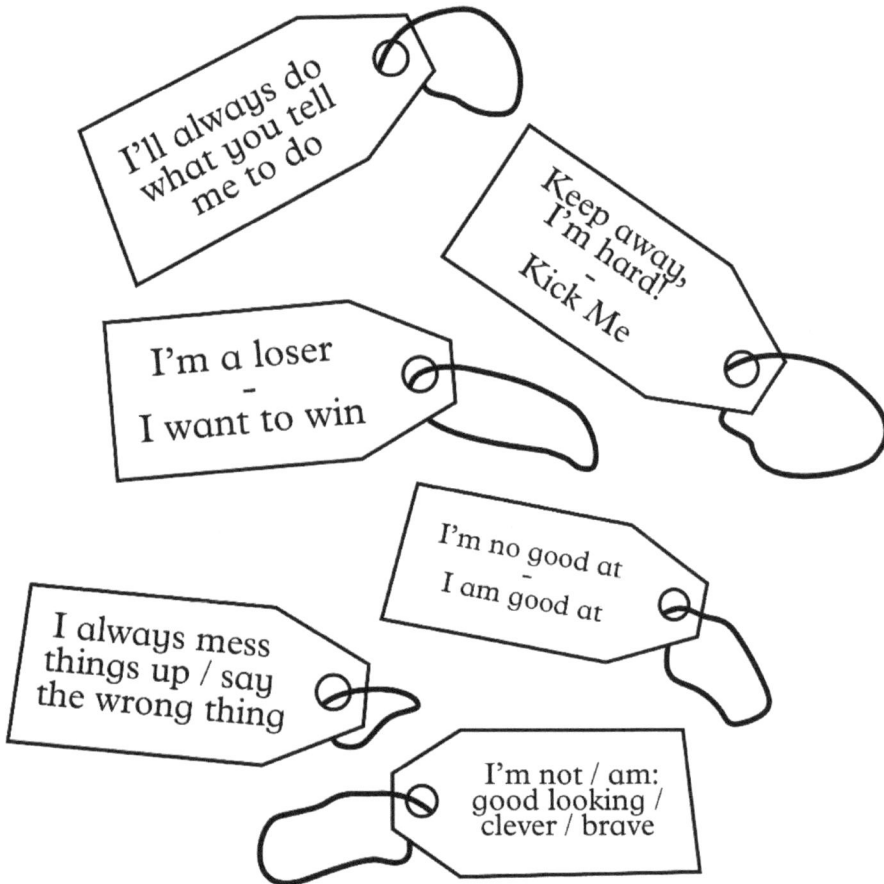

I'll always do what you tell me to do

Keep away, I'm hard! - Kick Me

I'm a loser - I want to win

I'm no good at - I am good at

I always mess things up / say the wrong thing

I'm not / am: good looking / clever / brave

Consider the following:

- In what situations might we see you living up to your label? Who are you with? How often does it happen? Where did you get this idea about yourself in the first place?

- Are these labels good/bad for you in any way? Why?

- Can labels be changed?

- Do the labels over-generalise or exaggerate (Is it true that you *always* mess up?)

- What evidence is there that you should wear each label?

Such questioning reveals that our inner voice is not only often inaccurate but can be harmful to our self-respect.

Section 3

THE INFLUENCE OF YOUR BELIEFS

We all develop a belief system, which begins early in our lives and continues as we get older. Some beliefs are very deep-seated, although we may not have articulated them clearly either to ourselves or to others; other beliefs are more conscious and very important to us; we may express these loudly and firmly. What you may not be aware of is the extent to which these beliefs influence you and your behaviour. We will look at aspects of behaviour in more detail later, but let's consider here three types of beliefs we all hold. (You can learn more about this by reading about Cognitive Behaviour Therapy theory (CBT)).

1. **Underlying 'rules'** or assumptions about how life 'should' be. (Catch yourself using *'should,'* *'ought'* or *'must'* and you're likely to find out what these are!) Examples include:
   - I 'must' do as I am told by authority figures
   - Life 'should' be fair for everyone
   - People 'ought' never to break promises

2. **Beliefs** about yourself, others, and the world in general. Do you recognise any of these types of statement?
   - 'I knew this would happen – I'm just too [stupid / unattractive / incompetent]'
   - 'That's typical of people like that' (maybe referring to class, background or education)
   - 'The world is a dangerous place'

3. **Messages from the past**

Do babies start off thinking negatively about themselves? Of course not! And yet, many people, by the time they start school, are already beginning to have doubts about themselves. Why does this happen? A lot of our beliefs about ourselves are formed because of what other people tell us. Early patterns, unless challenged, can last throughout our lives.

Here are some I can remember from my childhood:

You should learn to…

… grin and bear it

… take the rough with the smooth

… remember that someone is always worse off than you

… put others before yourself

Can you list any sayings, 'rules,' or advice that may have had a negative influence on your self-esteem?

Of course, very often there's a kind of self-fulfilling prophesy built in here: if you think or expect something, it seems more likely to come true. But is this just because you tend to give greater credence to things which support your beliefs? For example, if you believe you aren't attractive, when someone rejects you, you perceive this as 'proof' your belief is right.
Uncovering our beliefs involves looking more deeply at patterns in our thinking and behaviour.

Exercise: identify some underlying beliefs

Some underlying beliefs stem from your early life and upbringing. Make a list of things you learnt as a child, and perhaps never questioned, about how to behave. This could include admonitions you received or beliefs that developed through your own experience of how the world seemed to be. Do you still believe they are right?

Here are some examples that may feel familiar:

1	If I said what I wanted it would be selfish. You should always put others before yourself
2	I shouldn't burden people with my problems
3	It might be embarrassing or cause trouble if I say what I think
4	If I ask for what I want, and the other person says 'no,' it would mean they don't love me
5	I shouldn't have to say what I feel; if (s)he really loved me, (s)he'd know what I want
6	I have to pretend don't really mind (when I do!)
7	I expect it'll all work out in the end; why worry?
8	People shouldn't express negative feelings

9	If I express my disagreement/disapproval I might harm our relationship
10	I should always be able, successful, and 'on top of things' (if I'm not, I'm inadequate/ incompetent/ a failure)
11	It is important that everyone should like me
12	There's nothing I can do about problems - it's best just to ignore them and get on with it/ take the rough with the smooth
13	I need someone - often a specific person - to be with and lean on (I can't live happily by myself)
14	I don't like to make a fuss
15	Don't feel sorry for yourself - there are lots of people worse off than you

If you identify with any of these, you may also begin to see how they influence your behaviour. For example, you may be used to resigning yourself to situations you don't like, maybe feeling resentful later; you may avoid conflict and then find that your feelings are overlooked, and you feel neglected. Go through the list you made for this exercise and ask yourself:

- How has sticking to these rules/acting on these beliefs helped/hindered me?

- What do I actually believe now? Do I want to change or challenge any of these beliefs in the light of experience?
- If I were to write a list of my beliefs about life and living now, what would I include?

I embarked on this process many years ago, and I continually evaluate my ideas about how I want to live. One habit I've got into is:

1. If I feel a strong emotion or reaction to something *(e.g.: when an adult is shouting at a child)* – PAUSE
2. Work out what's going on, and why this is affecting me so much - is it because one of my core beliefs is being challenged? *(e.g.: it's important to treat everyone with respect)*
3. Is my reaction appropriate to the situation or am I overreacting? (This might relate to my emotional state – more of this later)
4. What options do I have in terms of how I respond? (Often based on another belief – *e.g.: 'you shouldn't interfere in other people's lives'*)

Later on, we will look at how beliefs affect our behaviour and our relationships, and you may decide you want to make some changes to your own belief system.

CULTURAL INFLUENCES

Imagine a new person comes into your life; this may be at work, within the family, within a friendship circle etc. How to you react to them at first? For example:

- Do you look at their appearance: what they wear, makeup, tattoos, jewellery etc?
- Do you want to know certain things about them – their home background, their relationships, their job etc. Why?
- Does the way they talk affect you at all?
- Is age relevant to how you initially feel about them?
- What cultural/ethnic features might cause a response in you?
- What physical aspects might draw your attention?

Are there any aspects of your own value system that might influence how you initially react to new people? To understand some of these responses, let's think about different aspects of the culture you were brought up in. Not all of the aspects below will be equally significant for you, but try to think how each of them might have affected who you are now and how you think.

Your birth family:

- What is/was your relationship with your parents like?
- Who's in charge in your family and how does this show?
- What roles do members of the family have?
- Who's the least likely to notice if you were upset and who's the most likely?
- How do people show that they care in your family?
- What traditions or routines have you taken from your family and what do you leave out (or wish you could leave out) and why?

Race and ethnicity: (Ethnicity includes nationality, language, regional culture etc)

- What messages about race and other differences did you take on board as a child growing up? What do you say to your children about these topics?
- What differences are you aware of between groups in your community and does this cause any challenges in your daily life?
- Are there any significant historical events within your cultural/ethnic history? How have these impacted on your family through the generations? (e.g.: wars, leaving your homeland, intermarrying)
- What wisdom and learning have been passed down from your predecessors?

Religion:

- How would you describe any religious beliefs you hold?
- Whether or not you have a conventional religious belief, what do you think we can learn from religions?

- Have you explored your beliefs about what happens when we die?
- What does spirituality mean to you?
- What happens when you are with someone whose religious beliefs are very different to your own?

Education:

- Is education considered important in your family and how has this family belief influenced you?
- What was your educational experience like? What are your views about the value of education for your children?
- Do you need a certain kind of education to be happy? Or have a good job?

Age:

(I've included age in this section because different cultures treat the ageing process differently and this will affect how you think about yourself and your own age at each different stage of life).

- In your birth family, were the children of different ages treated differently? What was your position and how did this affect you?
- How has your childhood experience influenced the sort of parent you are now? How do you feel your parenting will change as your children get older?
- What does getting older mean for you? How has this changed as you have progressed through life?
- How are older members of your family viewed by the younger members (and the other way around)?

SELF AND GENDER

Your sense of self and identity will include how you see yourself in terms of gender and sexuality. The following ideas and questions may help you clarify your thoughts and feelings about this aspect of your identity:

- Describe what being a man/woman means in your family (this may be your own family as an adult or the family you were brought up in)
- How do men show emotions and how do women show emotions?
- What are considered male/female roles in your family and how does this sit with you?
- Who taught you the most about being a man or woman in your family/in life in general?
- How do you respond to modern issues around gender?

Many writers such as John Gray (the 'Mars and Venus' man) suggest that traditional male/female roles are changing. Previously, the generally accepted norm was that women were the carers, and men the providers. This resulted in the attribution and valuing of certain characteristics in men, and others in women. These include:

Male attributes	Female attributes
Goal-oriented	Relationship oriented
Independent	Interdependent
Accountable	Emotional
Problem solver	Nurturer
Tough	Vulnerable
Competitive	Cooperative
Analytical	Intuitive
Powerful	Loving
Assertive	Trusting
Competent/confident	Virtuous

Nowadays, there is talk of males accessing their 'female' side and vice versa. Ideally, this results in a balance in which both males and females can feel more 'real', 'open' and valued. So, women might become more achievement- orientated, while still maintaining their loving side, while men can be more accepting of their emotions but still enjoy the fulfilment they get from success at work. Think about what this means for you:

- In what sense would you call yourself a 'typical' male/female?
- Have your views changed since you were a child?
- Do you feel that any part of your gender identity has not yet been fully explored and expressed?

YOUR HISTORY AND LIFELINE

As you will see from what we have talked about already, our history and experience have a huge influence on who we are today. A useful exercise is to look back over your life, by drawing a **lifeline**: Draw a straight horizontal line across a piece of paper. At one end, put a 0 (the start of your life) and at the other, your age now. Now think about the highs and lows of your life and when these took place. Go along the line and mark these in, above the line if they were good, under it if negative, labelling each event. You will end up with a kind of graph about your life experiences:

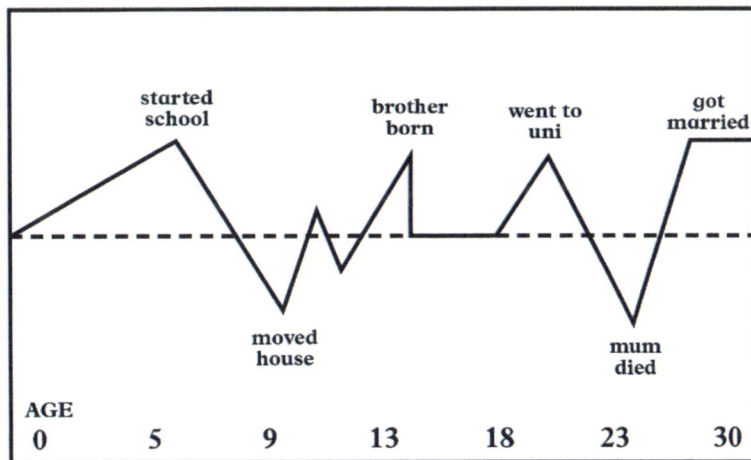

Think about the way these different experiences, responses and feelings have shaped your life, and made you who you are now. This can be so important in helping you to clarify your current priorities as well as your wishes for the future. It shows you what really mattered to you and affected you, so that you can be proactive in trying to bring into your life more of the experiences which you find rewarding and valuable.

Section 4

CONNECTING ASPECTS OF EXPERIENCE

Having explored a bit about the person you are today, we're going to go below the surface in order to look at how different aspects of experience interact. If we think of our bodies as a series of systems, we can recognise how something that happens in one part (e.g.: your brain) affects other parts such as the nervous system, your emotions, your physical sensations, and your behaviour. Clearly, this is very complex, involving all the parts that make up our physical and mental experiences. This simplified diagram shows how, when we experience something, a whole range of reactions happen:

An **event** takes place, which causes a series of **responses** in our:

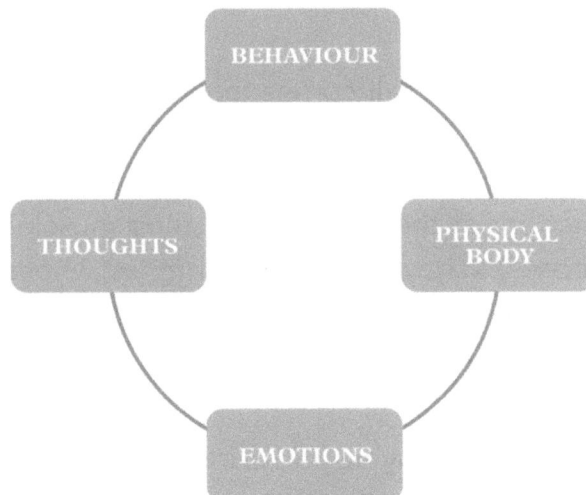

```
                    ┌──────────────┐
                    │  BEHAVIOUR   │
                    └──────────────┘

   ┌──────────────┐                    ┌──────────────┐
   │   THOUGHTS   │                    │   PHYSICAL   │
   │              │                    │     BODY     │
   └──────────────┘                    └──────────────┘

                    ┌──────────────┐
                    │   EMOTIONS   │
                    └──────────────┘
```

These are influenced by:
Context, previous experience, values and beliefs, and possibly other factors, such as genetics, age, mental and physical health, and levels of awareness. Below is an example of how these responses interact:

Example:

EMOTIONAL REACTIONS

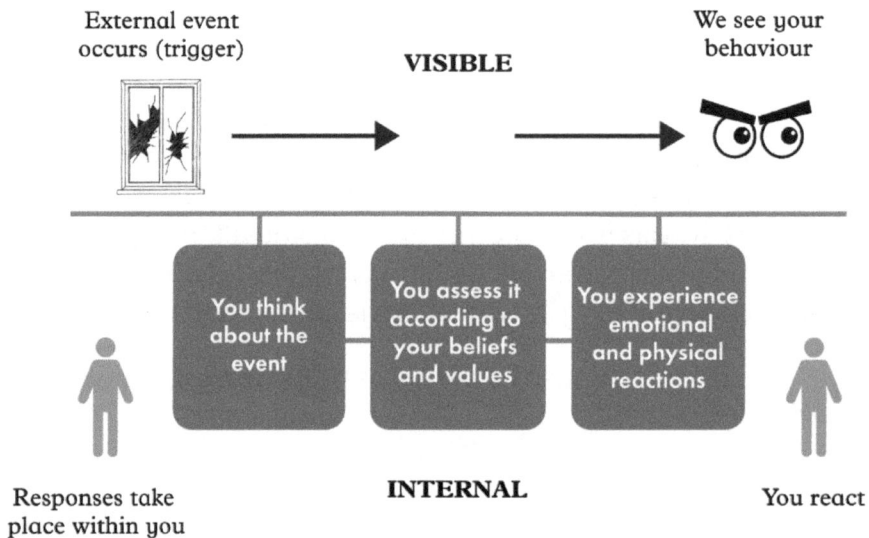

External event occurs (trigger)

VISIBLE

We see your behaviour

You think about the event

You assess it according to your beliefs and values

You experience emotional and physical reactions

Responses take place within you

INTERNAL

You react

So, in this example, a football comes through someone's window. His/her first **thoughts** are about how dreadful the perpetrator is, how unfair life is to him/her, etc. According to their belief system, no-one should behave like this. They get 'hot under the collar,' tense their muscles and start to shake. (**Physical** responses). They probably shout at whoever happens to be around. This is an aggressive **behaviour** style! (But…guess what…I bet they feel worse after this behaviour!)

The behavioural aspect of any response includes the visible expression of an **emotion**, such as a smile, a laugh, or something more extreme like aggression or running away. The way we show emotion is partly determined by the way feelings are shown within the society and culture that we live in, and the way we were brought up. We need to be aware that it is easy to misunderstand people who express themselves in a different way from ourselves. For more about emotion, see Section 7, page 47.

Section 5

THINKING STYLES

One of the most damaging things we do to ourselves, usually without realising it, is to allow unhelpful thinking patterns to colour our experience of the world.

It can be helpful to remember how our thoughts, feelings and behaviours are all connected. Some psychologists use the ABC model[2]:

A represents the '**activating event**' – the trigger or cause of the reaction
B refers to the way your **beliefs** influence how you respond
C is the **consequence**, (emotional, physical, and behavioural,) of A and B working together

For example:
A: the barman ignores you and serves other people who have been waiting less time (A)
B: Your belief system states that everyone should treat you fairly (B)
C: You become tense, feel angry at the way you are treated, and storm out (C)

Often, the situation is much more complicated than this, but what we are interested in at the moment is how your underlying beliefs affect the way you think, and how **distorted or unhelpful thinking** can get in the way of your enjoyment of life. After an event takes place, almost immediately, you experience a (unique) response. At stage B, you can probably identify the thoughts that go through your mind at a conscious level, though you may not be aware of the deeper beliefs that influence these thoughts. For example, you may think: 'I can't stand being ignored', 'That barman is a …' and so on (at a deeper level you may believe that *people should never be unfair*). Your thoughts, coupled with an emotional and physical reaction, feed your behavioural response.
Observing your thinking over time can help to show up patterns. Certain types of thinking can be unhelpful to your general wellbeing, and it is worth

looking at your thought patterns to see which negative/unhelpful tendencies you have. This can help to explain why sometimes you have an emotional reaction which seems 'too big' for the situation: something has acted as a **trigger** for feelings which can seem very powerful, but which other people might react to much less strongly (because they don't share the same beliefs, expectations, or past as you). The personal meaning you attach to reality could distort your understanding. Remember too, that this can affect your physical wellbeing – you may show symptoms of stress, for instance.

UNHELPFUL THINKING

CBT practitioners identify a number of different types of unhelpful thinking, some of which you may recognise in yourself. Thoughts and beliefs are of course closely linked, and often thoughts serve to confirm or support underlying beliefs. Have a look at these and see if they strike a chord with you:

Type of thinking	Example
Only noticing the negative aspects of situations	My friend ignored me: she doesn't like me anymore. The house is untidy: I can't cope.
Making judgements based on my beliefs	I blame the other person/people involved. People are so thoughtless.
Predicting the future and anticipating difficulties	The future seems black. I will never be able to get over this.

Mind-reading: assuming I know what others are thinking (and they know what I'm thinking!)	This is a bad sign because it means *x* doesn't like me. Everyone will think I'm incapable after this.
Catastrophising: imagining the worst possible outcome	This is so dreadful, I can't cope. I made a huge mistake: I'll be sacked
Self-criticising: blaming or shaming ourselves	This means I am a bad person. I'm a complete failure. I deserve to be severely punished for this/not to be forgiven.
Black-and-white thinking: seeing things in terms of extremes such as right/wrong	My whole life is a disaster. Things will never go right. You're either good or bad.
Should/must/ought: thoughts that come from underlying beliefs	(S)he should have known better. I ought to be able to cope.
Confusing here-and-now with memories	When this happened before, I was really upset/helpless so I can't deal with it now.
Emotional thinking: allowing difficult feelings to affect how you experience events now	I feel really scared so this situation must be threatening. I feel like a fraud so I must be one.

By exploring thinking patterns, you may begin to realise that your thoughts influence what happens in your life, and your self-esteem, more than you realise. Because of how you think, you will have some positive and some negative ways of behaving both towards yourself and in relationships. Many people find it useful to think in terms of a metaphor which helps them understand the influence of their negative thinking patterns. Some refer to their *'inner critic'* or *'internal bully'* or imagine *'the poisoned parrot'* who sits on their shoulder feeding their negativity. You could even give a name to the negative voice in your head!

Try answering these questions to see how positively you behave towards yourself.

Score 0 for not at all, 1 for only a little, up to 5 for often/usually.

I feel good about how I look	
I am good at lots of things, and use my talents	
I can easily ask for what I want	
I look after my body	
I make my own choices	
I can accept praise graciously	
I can handle criticism	
I believe people enjoy talking to me	
My sense of humour sees me through many situations	
I reward myself when I deserve it	
I accept help when I need it	
I forgive myself when I make mistakes	

I get over things quickly when they go wrong	
I keep difficulties in proportion	
I treat myself and others with respect	
When I'm learning something new, I persevere	
I celebrate my successes and achievements	
I know my faults and I can live with them	
I don't need to impress other people	
I'm not afraid to ask for help when I need it	

Section 6

UNDERSTANDING YOUR BEHAVIOUR STYLE

It would be an over-generalisation to say that any of us behave in the same way all the time. However, it is useful to look at behaviour in terms of certain styles that have been described by psychologists, with which most of us can identify. Some major styles and their characteristics are as follows:

Style of behaviour	Characteristics
Aggressive	• Domineering • Seeking personal gain at others' expense • Competitive • Attacking • May use verbal or physical abuse
Passive	• Gives in easily • Avoids responsibility • Sees self as victim • Puts self down • Gives credit to others

Manipulative/passive-aggressive/indirectly aggressive	• Indirectly controlling e.g.: sulks • Lacks trust so 'tests' people • Can be deceitful • Tries to influence you in an indirect way – e.g.: the martyr induces guilt, so you'll do what (s)he wants
Assertive	• Able to ask for what (s)he wants/say no to what (s)he doesn't want • Can express him/herself and his/her feelings clearly and calmly and be listened to. • Behaves in a controlled, confident way • Can communicate effectively with a range of people • Deals effectively with disagreements and conflicts • Able to say and hear 'no' and handle criticism

Often, it is possible to tell which style someone is using by observing their verbal (words used, tone of voice etc.) and non-verbal (facial expression, eye contact, body language) behaviour.

ASSERTIVENESS

How can learning to be assertive help us in our everyday lives? The word assertiveness describes a pattern or style of behaviour which enables us to communicate effectively with people.

We are able to be open and honest, while at the same time respecting others' rights. A person who is assertive can:

- Stand up for him/herself
- Ensure his/her feelings or opinions are considered
- State clearly what (s)he expects or wants
- Act with integrity and respect, towards him/herself and others
- Be direct and honest, avoiding playing games
- Be aware of choices, make choices and take responsibility for these
- Develop and improve relationships with others, even in difficult situations
- Accept disappointment and refusals
- Live his/her life without dependency on the approval of others
- Communicate thoughts, feelings and beliefs in an open, honest manner, without violating the rights of others
- Avoid being *aggressive* (where they might abuse others' rights) or *passive* (abusing their own rights)

Explore your behaviour styles

Since much of our behaviour follows patterns, it's worth looking at your own behaviour and considering whether it would be helpful to make any changes to your usual ways of behaving. It may be that you can identify times when you react passively or aggressively, where a more assertive approach would be more helpful.

In the following exercise, fill in your responses to various situations. You may not have experienced exactly these, but perhaps something similar has happened to you.

The point of the exercise is to learn about how you deal with uncomfortable situations. Try to identify the ones where you behave assertively, passively, or aggressively. Also consider what underlies your behaviour: the feelings and thoughts which lead you to act that way. This will help you focus on the kinds of situations in which it might help you to behave more assertively

Situation	Typical reaction from me (thoughts, feelings, behaviour)	Is this assertive, passive, or aggressive?
You lent a friend some money a few weeks ago and she hasn't returned it. You very much need it back now.		
In a restaurant the service is poor, and your meal is not cooked well.		
A colleague at work who is the opposite sex says something personal about your appearance.		
Your boss dumps a lot of new work on you close to home time.		
The assistant in the shop insists that the item of clothing you are thinking of buying is just right for you, but you have doubts.		
Someone you know only slightly pays you a compliment.		

Situation	Typical reaction from me (thoughts, feelings behaviour)	Is this assertive, passive or aggressive?
You partner has a habit which really irritates you, and you would feel a lot better if he/she would stop it.		
Once again, everybody has gone out/upstairs and left you with a huge mess to clear up.		
You are given some criticism at work which you feel is not justified.		
Your mother-in-law wants to come for the weekend, and you don't want her to.		
Someone pushes in front of you in the queue.		
A friend rings you at half-past six wanting a baby-sitter.		
Put in a situation of your own which occurs fairly often.		

After this, you may begin to realise what kinds of situations are most difficult for you. For instance, they may involve:
- Expressing feelings, needs or wants
- Saying no
- Handling criticism or potential conflict
- Taking responsibility

Look at some behaviour patterns you have developed, especially around situations such as the following, and consider whether or not these have been helpful to you:

Dealing with 'unacceptable' feelings
Some people find certain feelings difficult to deal with. These may include anger, dislike or hate, and envy. When you experience any of these, how do you deal with them? Are you likely to express them openly and address them in a helpful way? Or do you defend against them in some way?

Dealing with undesirable impulses
You may have from time to time all sorts of 'secret' wishes or desires, from doing physical harm to someone, to wanting to shout and scream, to having more lurid fantasies! To live comfortably in society, we need to deal with these effectively, but not everyone can do this, and some of us allow such impulses to affect their behaviour and wellbeing. Do you do this?

Defending against fears and anxieties
When you think about fears you have, particularly in relation to other people, do you respond to these in a 'healthy' way, or do you defend against them? For example, how do you handle anxiety about loneliness or feeling different and not being accepted? What about fear of being hurt and let down? We all have favourite defences, from denial to projection (blaming others).

Why are some people more assertive than others?
The ability to behave in an assertive way is connected to our levels of self-esteem or confidence. As we've already seen, beliefs about ourselves, which contribute to levels of self-esteem, often originate from when we were growing up - the things people around us taught us, and our environment - the media, peer pressure and other influences. Adults who lack confidence can often track this back to early bullying or ridicule or a very controlling

environment. They may have learnt to act passively or aggressively to protect themselves or to try to earn approval ('people pleasing'). Similarly, today, many young people are preoccupied with how they are perceived on social media. They can be very reliant on 'likes' and may even distort their portrayal of themselves in order to feel accepted. This creation of a '**false self**' is very damaging to self-esteem and erodes confidence rather than enhancing it.

When we behave in non-assertive ways, it may be because we hold beliefs such as those we looked at on pages 21 and 22, including:

- We mustn't upset or burden other people
- It would be terrible to be rejected
- I must fight people who mistreat me

Do you recognise any of these in your own thinking? But consider what happens if you *don't* behave assertively:

If you are too **passive,** you give out at least some of the following messages:
my feelings and needs aren't as important as yours
I'll put up with anything
I'll do anything to avoid losing/hurting you

All of which could lead to
- people exploiting or taking advantage of you
- people ignoring or overlooking you
- your wishes not being taken into consideration

On the other hand, if you are **aggressive** the outcomes of your behaviour can include:
- making enemies/causing others to avoid you
- being unable to relax/being constantly on the defensive
- having relationships that are unstable
- facing consequences such as punishment for violence

Passive-aggressive people try to control the behaviour of others by playing games, sulking etc.:
Of course I'm alright, leave me alone (when you're clearly not)
OK - I'll do it then (when you don't want to)

I've sacrificed so much for you!
This means:
- their relationships aren't based on genuine communication
- problems go unresolved because they aren't confronted
- a distance develops between them and others

What would you like to do in a more assertive way?
Let's take a quick look at some of the difficult situations that assertive behaviour could help us with:

Uncomfortable Feelings
What feelings do you find it difficult to express? Often, people will cite anger as an example; you might wish to include other feelings such as disappointment or dislike. You may have been taught, when you were younger, to suppress some of these feelings.

How do you behave when you are feeling something strongly, but you find it really hard to tell the other person? Some of us overreact and get aggressive; some behave childishly; some try to forget about it but let the resentment fester. The feelings are still there however and can be triggered sometimes by things which remind us of previous situations when they occurred – so we have '**hot-spots**' or **triggers** which other people may not recognise. Bottled up feelings also have a tendency to build and build until there's an explosion! An increasing weight of negative feeling may lead to a person becoming depressed, having an effect rather like a poison inside them.

It would be much better if these emotions could be dealt with as and when they arise. To become more aware of your feelings, so it is easier to express them, a starting point is simply to name your feelings in a given situation. For instance, on the anger scale, where does your feeling fit? Are you *furious* or just *disappointed…really upset*, or *a bit sad*…? This will help in your decision-making about what to do next. See page 51 for more help.

Dealing with criticism
Some criticism, even if it feels hurtful, can be helpful; it gives us an insight into how we are perceived by other people and allows us the opportunity to change unhelpful behaviour if we so wish. Most of us would be glad if we could learn to do something better, or to treat someone in a way that makes

it more comfortable for both of us. So, learning to receive this kind of criticism in an assertive way would be of great benefit.

Other types of criticism are less helpful, and intended either to damage us, or to boost the feelings of someone else at our expense. It is valuable to learn to distinguish between the two. If you can see when criticism is more about the other person and their efforts to boost their own confidence, you will feel better. Examples might be when they label you in a negative way (*'You're useless'*), are patronising (*'That's quite good - for you'*), or they even just ignore you. Look out for this in your day-to-day dealings with others and only accept criticism you believe to be justified. Learn to apologise when it's appropriate and you will feel much better.

Saying 'no'

How many of these ways of dealing with unwelcome requests do you recognise in yourself?

- Do you ever tend to give a vague response that might make the other person think they could persuade you if they persist?
- Do you feel under pressure to reply at once, so don't really think the situation through?
- Do you try to justify your responses by giving reasons why you are refusing (*'I'm busy on Thursday'*) and does this actually supply them with ammunition for an argument? (*'Oh, well how about Friday?'*)

Explore your reluctance to say no and try to understand what you have difficulty with if you identify with this. If you find yourself struggling to say no to people, you might ask why this is so difficult. A lot of the reluctance to refuse a request may spring from beliefs we hold, as described above. In addition, it is well-known that gaining praise and love from other people (e.g.: our parents in childhood) contributes hugely to building our self-esteem. So, as children, we behaved as our mums or dads wanted us to. To an extent, this makes for harmonious living.

The problem is that if we become so conditioned to being 'good' and **pleasing others**, we don't know how to get in touch with what we actually want and feel, or express a view that disagrees with someone else. This can mean we spend an awful lot of time doing things we don't want to do, with people we don't want to be with. Are you a 'people-pleaser'? If so, what are you scared will happen if you refuse someone?

Dealing with conflict and grievances

What do you do when an argument threatens? Which of these statements fits how you behave when you feel a potential conflict arising?

- I will do anything to avoid an argument
- I tend to take on the role of: collaborator, peacemaker, arbitrator, audience/listener, fighter
- I feel defensive and start to plan my counterattack
- I need to win the battle/prove I'm right/punish the other person
- I would compromise my needs and wishes to keep the peace but expect the other person to 'pay me back' for doing this
- I always hope the outcome of a disagreement will be a win-win situation where both parties feel listened to and respected
- I want someone to rescue me and sort it out

Again, at this stage, the aim is to help you to get to know yourself better by observing your behaviour and understanding what it's about. You can probably already see the potential for changing the bits you're not happy about, and we'll explore how to do this in Section 12, page 87.

Section 7

WORKING WITH YOUR EMOTIONS

Emotions probably affect your mental wellbeing more than anything else. In recent years, a great deal of scientific research has been done into how emotions are connected to our physical and mental wellbeing, moods and behaviour. It is worth pausing here to look at some of the things we know about how emotions affect our lives.

(Note that here I am using the words *emotions* and *feelings* interchangeably, although you will come across writers who make a distinction between the two. Also be aware that there is a difference between an emotion and a mood: a mood can last for hours, days, or even weeks, perhaps at a low level, without you really knowing why; it can influence perception, motivation, decision-making and social interactions. Your mood, particularly if it's a negative mood, starts to get in the way of your work and family life, then it can become a problem doctors call a mood disorder.)

What are emotions?
1. **The scientific view**

Recent studies in neuroscience (see bibliography) have helped us to understand what goes on in our brain, and then our body, when we respond emotionally to an external stimulus. In trying to understand our emotions, a good place to start is by looking at how part of our brain works. When something is perceived in the outside world, the fastest response takes place in the **limbic system** (sometimes called the *'mammalian brain'*):

THE LIMBIC SYSTEM

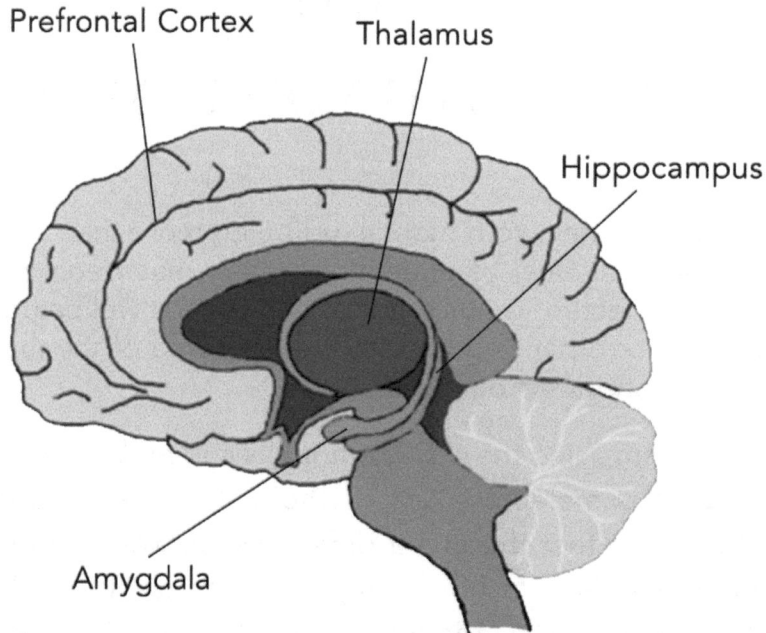

1. The **thalamus** receives the sensory input (sounds, sights etc)
2. The **amygdala** interprets the significance of these perceptions to determine whether there is any threat to survival
3. This process is aided by the **hippocampus**, where memories are stored

If a threat is detected, a message goes rapidly to the **hypothalamus** and the *'reptilian brain'* – the **brain stem**, prompting the secretion of the hormones **cortisol** and **adrenalin**, which in turn stimulate the **autonomic nervous system** (leading to a whole-body response – rapid breathing, heart rate and blood pressure etc), to prepare us for:

FIGHT OR FLIGHT

Meanwhile, the message from the thalamus also moves, slightly more slowly, to the *'new brain'*: the **neocortex** and more specifically, the **prefrontal cortex** within this. This is largely where rational thought happens, and this can result in a tempering of the initial strong reaction. This enables you to decide whether the danger is real; if not, the stress response will gradually subside. You can then make an appropriate choice about how to act.

The first, more immediate, response tends to be driven by emotions, such as fear: I see a spider, I jump and seek to escape. I have memories of seeing big black spiders running very fast! After the second, slower response has had time to kick in, I may be able to think more clearly: this little thing is not a threat to me and I can cope with it! All this is summarised in the diagram on page 50.

There are clear links between our behaviour and the 'emotional brain' and the 'rational' brain. Sometimes, we act on 'gut instinct' (an emotional response which precipitates a physical reaction - fast track) and sometimes we think things through carefully (slower route). Which course we take is partly dependent on past experiences, remembered by the hippocampus.

This is why, in helping with mental health, we need to look at both logical and rational ways of understanding situations, and also at which emotions are evoked, and their meaning for the individual concerned, in any given situation. Controlling stress and managing emotional difficulties requires balancing both the emotional and the rational.

The good news is that, because the brain is plastic, new ways of responding can be learnt, to replace unhelpful responses. So, for example, with the right help, social anxiety can be overcome, and old, unhelpful patterns gradually replaced.

BRAIN RESPONSES

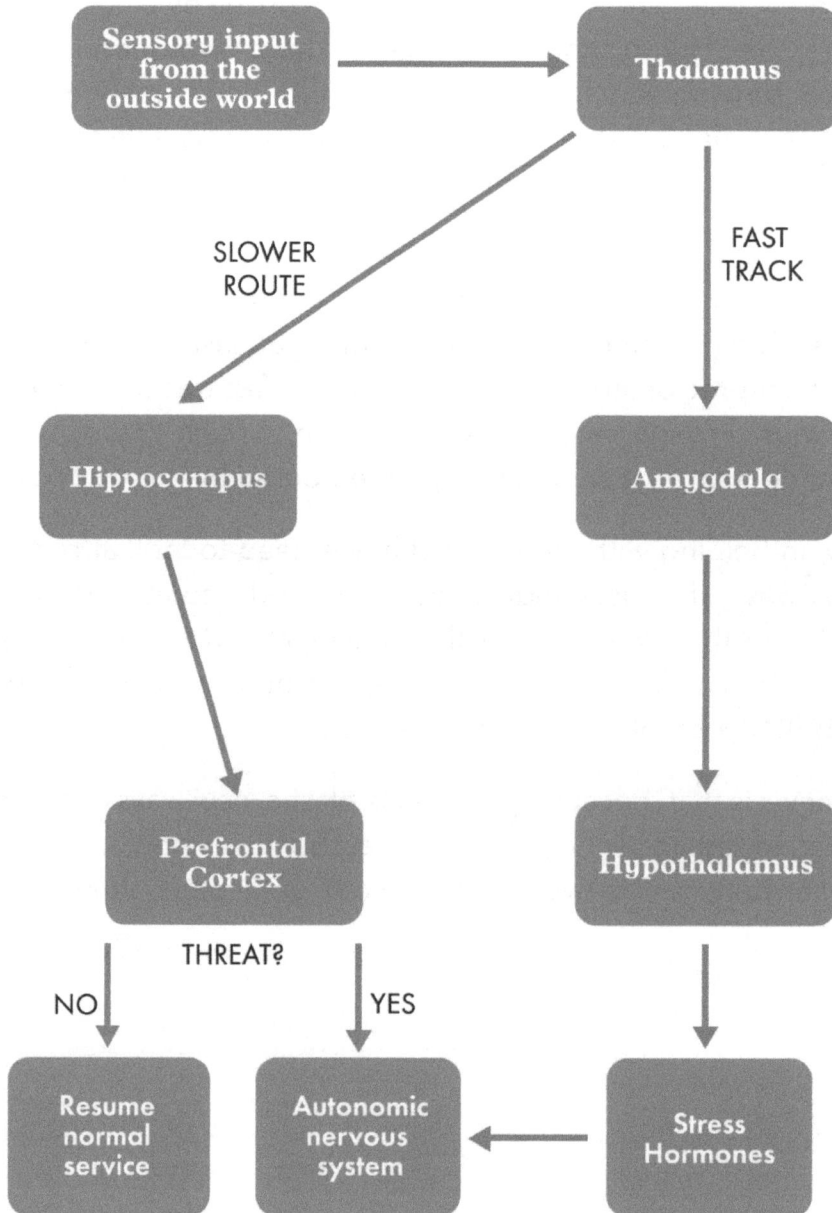

While basic emotions are universal and may be expressed by all of us, the responses to the experiences that produce them can he highly subjective. Each individual may feel differently in response to apparently similar experiences (getting married, losing a loved one). Because you and your past experiences are unique, what applies to you will not be the same for another person. So, for example, if you've previously been in a car crash, someone cutting you up is likely to make you react more strongly than someone who has never had this experience.

An individual's emotional history is especially important: if you had, for example, a happy, loving childhood, you will be more able to make good relationships with new people. But if your caregivers were often angry, fearful emotions might make you more anxious around new people.

Sometimes your brain can trigger an emotion unconsciously. This means that your brain might react to something in a situation and trigger an emotional response, without you even noticing it. Have you ever had that feeling of a kind of growing anxiety when you're talking to someone, but you don't really know why? It could be that the person reminds you (at a subconscious level) of someone who upset you in the past; you may become angry with them without really knowing why. (If I hear a particular type of voice, it reminds me, largely unconsciously, of an especially critical teacher; someone else might not find anything awkward about the person concerned). This shows that your reactions are unique and individual to you.

In addition, although certain external signs can be understood (the red face and fist clenching of an angry person), because emotions are largely subjective, they can be difficult to describe and understand; even more than this: it can be hard to understand and empathise with other people's emotions. (If I asked you 'What do you mean by sadness?' you might find it hard to put into words, although you would probably be able to give examples of when you personally have experienced sadness; your description, however, would not be the same as mine).

It helps to know your own '**hot-spots**' or **triggers.** Our nervous system gets fired up ('fight, flight, or freeze') to respond to triggers, which in turn causes a range of physiological changes, such as the release of stress hormones and an increase of blood pressure. In the short term, these changes can help us cope with a problem, but over time, stress hormones can be being damaging to our bodies if we are unable either to express, process or calm the emotions which led to their secretion. You will have certain triggers that cause you to react strongly; if you know what these are, you can either avoid them or practise better ways to deal with them.

QUIZ – YOUR TRIGGERS?

Score these emotional situations from 0 – 5 according to how badly they may affect you. (You may have examples of your own that fit in the second column)

Type of Emotion	Triggering Event	Score
Feeling rejected	Someone leaving you.	
	Failure to get a job.	
	Someone ignoring you.	
Feeling frightened	Having to do something on your own.	
	Being with people you don't know.	
	Being with people in authority.	
	Worrying about health conditions.	
Feeling controlled	Someone forcing their attention on you.	
	Someone trying to stop you doing what you want.	
	Someone 'smothering' you emotionally.	
Feeling let down	Someone doesn't do something they promised.	
	You work hard but don't get what you deserve.	

Feeling criticised	Someone giving you a disapproving look.	
	Someone blaming or shaming you.	
	Someone being judgemental towards you.	
Feeling angry	Someone abusing your rights.	
	Someone damaging something of yours.	
	Someone being unkind to someone you love.	
Feeling overwhelmed	Feeling helpless in a difficult situation.	
	Being asked to do something you haven't been trained for.	
	Getting lost.	

2. Links with behaviour

The last part of an emotional reaction is that you start to want to behave in a particular way. For example, if you are angry, you might want to yell or fight with someone; if you are scared, you might feel a strong desire to run away. Or, if you are sad, you may just want to avoid people and not talk to anyone.

When behaviour is driven by emotions, and your thinking brain isn't able to help you to be rational, there can be real problems in controlling your behaviour. (People talk about 'the red mist' for example).

4. Other factors

In addition to what we have seen about the functioning of our brain and body, and about how we interpret things in a subjective way, questions arise about **nature versus nurture.** Some of the findings of recent research have explored whether our **genes** influence our behaviour. For instance, are some people more naturally predisposed towards anger than others? It has been found that certain genes produce an enzyme which affects the neurotransmitters dopamine and serotonin. It was thought low levels of this enzyme may cause people to be impulsive or even aggressive; however, most scientists agree that so many other factors are involved, especially the kind of upbringing we had, that the significance of this is relatively small. (See bibliography: Frazzetto)

How does our **environment** affect us? Our upbringing and any traumatic experiences (such as abuse or neglect) will seriously affect our mental health and our behaviour in a whole variety of ways. Those who have been the victims of violence are likely to demonstrate violent behaviour themselves.

It is interesting, if you have never done it, to create a **genogram**[3] for your family. This is like a family tree, but rather than focusing simply on relationships, you look at behaviour and events within the members' lives. I once did this with a friend and we discovered that, for at least three generations, a single female child had given birth outside wedlock. Often, you might find tendencies such as alcoholism or other risky behaviour are repeated through the generations.

EMOTIONAL AWARENESS

In order to understand, process and manage your own emotions, you first need to practise becoming more **aware** of them so that you can identify what you are feeling and why; you can then learn to help yourself deal with difficult feelings. A starting point for this is to learn a whole range of words for emotions and to use them to be more specific about just what is going on for you at any given time. There are lots of examples of lists of emotions, and I also like to look at an 'emotions wheel.' There are lots of these available online.

At the centre, you can see what are often considered the four major emotions. As you work towards the outside of the circle, you will see more specific words for various degrees and nuances of these; the outside ring tends to include some of the most powerful feelings that are related to the central ones. You can use this to develop an emotional vocabulary.

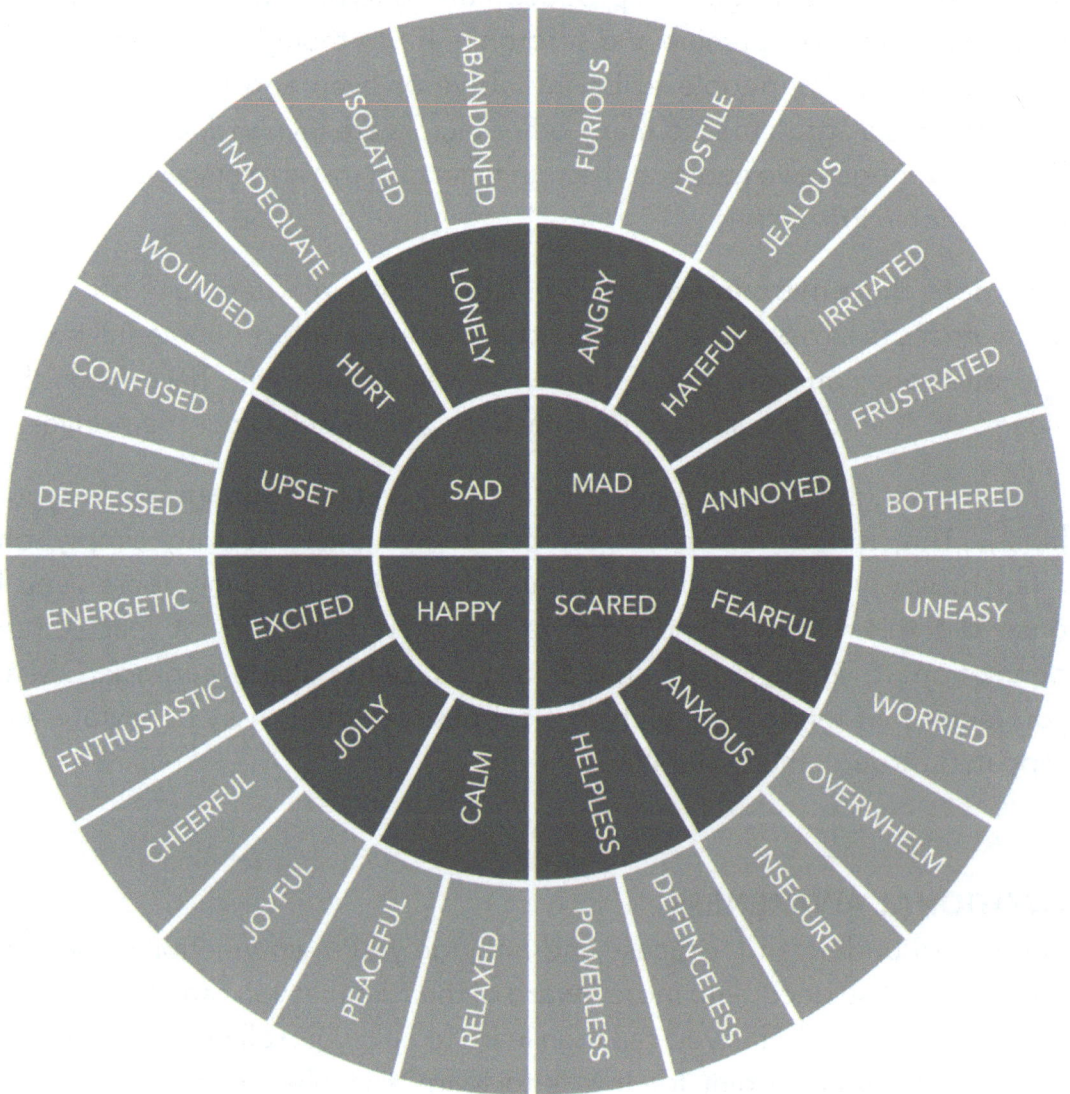

So, how good are you at naming and describing your feelings?

Answer true or false to these statements:

- I am clear about my feelings
- I pay attention to how I feel
- I often experience emotions which seem overwhelming
- When I am upset, I feel angry with myself/embarrassed

- I find it difficult to 'open up' about my deep feelings

And answer these general questions:

- What kinds of feelings do you experience most often in your life?
- Which emotions do you express openly most and least often?
- Does the idea of exploring your emotions with another person make you feel uncomfortable?

We could sum up the process of becoming aware of emotions and their accompanying effects as a process which follows various stages:

1. Notice the feeling.
2. Name the emotion: What is it? What words best describe what you are feeling?
3. Accept the emotion. It's a normal bodily reaction.
4. Try to understand how it came about - what set of circumstances contributed to you feeling this way?
5. Investigate the emotion. How intensely do you feel it? Notice physical sensations: how are you breathing? What are you feeling in your body? Where do you feel it? What's your facial expression?
6. Identify any thoughts that come into your mind.
7. Notice what you want to do (e.g.: fight or flight).

You need to be able to feel and recognise a range of emotions, but *extremes* of emotion can cause problems. Sadness can become depression, anger can become aggression, and excess pleasure can lead to addiction. Feeling afraid in a dangerous situation is natural and useful. But being too fearful can cause unhelpful anxiety, phobias, and panic attacks. However, *suppression* of behavioural and emotional responses has also been found to be harmful to your wellbeing. This is partly why those in the emergency services need to debrief after a traumatic incident.

The ability to recognise, understand and **manage** our own emotions and the behaviour that is associated with them, and to understand the feelings and behaviour of others, has become known as **emotional intelligence**.

MANAGING YOUR EMOTIONS

How good are you at managing your emotions and their consequent behaviour? Therapists helping with difficult emotions often ask their clients to keep a record of times during their week when strong emotions have seemed difficult to control. For example, they may look at a scenario where someone became very angry. The therapist then asks them to examine the circumstances surrounding powerful emotional experiences, perhaps by completing a record sheet like the following:

Describe where you were/what you were doing	
What was the event that prompted your strong reaction?	
Name the emotions you felt as accurately as you can	
How intense (scale 1-10) were your emotions?	
What physical sensations did you experience?	
What were your thoughts at the time?	
How did you behave/what did you do?	
Were you trying to communicate something/influence someone else	
After it was over, what did you think/feel and how long did the effects last?	
How are you feeling about it now?	
Anything else you became aware of?	

We have talked a lot about the connection between thoughts, feelings, behaviour, and physical sensations. You can see how all of these are interlinked here. See Section 13, page 115 for more about managing feelings.

It is important to repeat at this stage that emotions are *normal*! There is nothing intrinsically wrong with feeling angry and often this is perfectly justified and can lead to us seeking to improve something in society. Nevertheless, if an emotion or the way you express it is causing problems for you, e.g., if your anger is leading to relationship problems or if you seem to be feeling sad for most of the time, you might like to consider whether there are any changes you can make to your behaviour or your situation which might help to improve your life. This is the subject of the second part of this book, although addressing more specific mental health problems such as depression and anxiety needs to be done separately.

Section 8

HOW HAPPY ARE YOU?

At the end of this exploration of who you are, let's consider, keeping in mind all you have learnt about yourself, what actually makes you happy, and whether you are getting enough of it. This final set of exercises can highlight the good things in your life as well as helping you to clarify what you would like to change about any aspect of your life so that you can improve your mental wellbeing.

1. **Finding balance:**
   - How often do you feel physically tired, and why?
   - What represents a good work/life balance for you? How much time do you spend away from work, engaged with people and activities you enjoy? It is useful to create a pie chart, to look at how you use your time, over any 24-hour period:

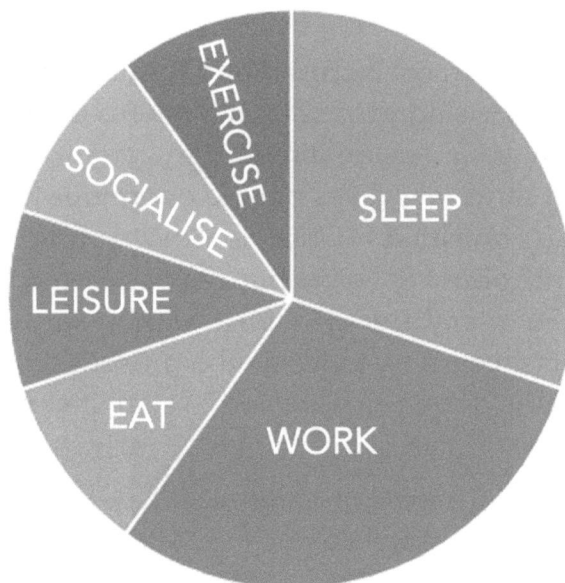

2. **What resources do you have and are you making good use of them?**

- Draw yourself at the centre of a large piece of paper then around this do drawings to represent people and things which **support** you. This can remind you how to access help, kindness, and company when you need it.
- Identify your **personal traits and qualities**. What do you or your friends like about you? In what ways do you feel good about the way you live your life and relate to those around you? If you passed on your three best qualities to your children, what would they be? Which characteristics help you in a crisis?
- List all the **skills** you have, both personal (e.g.: a good listener) and practical or work-related. If you have a job, what do you enjoy about it and how do you see your working future?
- List the **activities** you do for fun, pleasure, and relaxation.
- In what ways do you feel you have a **positive** way of seeing the world or thinking about what happens to you? Think of a single word to describe your thinking style (e.g.: *optimistic, cautious, realistic*…).

3. **Finding meaning in life:**

- Make a '**favourites** list': favourite…colours, activities, animals, etc.
- What do you do for a treat, however small (e.g., choosing your favourite food for tea, stroking a dog, listening to favourite music)? Do you actively try to do something that gives you pleasure as regularly as you can?
- When have you felt most **inspired and fulfilled**? Is this to do with your role in the family, using your skills and talents or achieving something at work or in your leisure time? Very often, contributing to the community in some way gives people enormous fulfilment.
- What gives you **spiritual** nourishment? What feeds your soul? This is not necessarily about religion but resides in the here-and-now felt experience. For many, being in touch with beauty – art, music, nature – lifts the spirits. Learning to live in the present moment (some might say 'mindfully') is good practice, and to start, it's enough just to:

  STOP   BREATHE   BE STILL   LOOK   LISTEN   SMELL   TOUCH
- Are you clear about your priorities and hopes? Do you have a clear future pathway (where will you be in 1/3/5 years' time)?

THE PURSUIT OF HAPPINESS

I imagine that you read books like this because you want to be happy. In reality, it is unrealistic to expect to be constantly happy. For most people, happy states may be fleeting, mundane feelings occur a lot of the time, and difficulties and problems can sometimes cause low mood.

Not many people would be happy with a life of pure hedonism; there is something more satisfying about leading a life that involves the pursuit of other things - knowledge, family, creativity etc. as well as meaningful relationships within society. For many, mere pleasure-seeking represents selfishness and lack of moral restraint which can have a darker side (think of addiction!)

Ultimately, most of us will be reasonably content if we can arrive at a state of **homeostasis**, or balance, between pleasure and pain. So, can we influence the amount of happiness/pleasure or contentment in our lives?

What is happiness? An anatomical perspective on pleasure:

Apologies if this isn't your thing, but it can be fascinating to know what goes on in our bodies and brains when we experience emotions, so I'm going to say a little about what happens when we feel pleasure.

An area within the brain known as the **reward system** consists of various parts, which, when they work together, can stimulate the production of pleasure-inducing chemicals (see below) to give us feelings of joy and pleasure. A very brief summary of the process involved is as follows:

As we already know, when a stimulus is received, (i.e.: something you like in the environment is perceived), **the prefrontal cortex** evaluates this by comparing this experience to memories of what we have found rewarding in the past. If something is judged to be potentially rewarding (note that this is in *anticipation* of something pleasant occurring) the next stage takes place: the cortex sends signals to the **ventral tegmental area.**

The ventral tegmental area responds to sensation signals by flooding the **nucleus accumbens** and other regions in the system with the neurotransmitter **dopamine**, a hormone associated with pleasure (neurotransmitters send messages between different parts of the brain). The nucleus accumbens receives these pleasure-messages and sends out (via neurons) further messages to various other parts of the brain and the nervous system. This generates responses we associate with feelings of happiness, like laughter and euphoria.

If we experience something as rewarding, we are likely to repeat it, which can help for example with survival e.g.: eating and activity connected with reproduction. It could be argued then, that emotions such as happiness, are nothing more than motivators that enhance an organism's chances of survival!

THE PLEASURE CHEMICALS

We feel joy in our bodies because of the release of dopamine and serotonin, two types of neurotransmitters which influence our emotional and physiological experiences. Both of these chemicals are closely associated with happiness.

Dopamine is a neurotransmitter that plays a big part in how we feel pleasure. It affects many aspects of our behaviour and mental functions, such as motivation, mood and learning, and plays a role in directing our attention, helping us to determine what is significant in our experience of our environment. It's also part of our human ability to think and plan and respond with interest to something. (If you feel passionately about something, your system is probably generating a lot of dopamine). When I was younger, I remember agony aunts on problem pages always seemed to be suggesting that unhappy people should get a hobby. While this may sound old-fashioned, it makes sense if you want to increase your dopamine levels! Dopamine is also enhanced by diet and exercise. However, its pleasure-seeking effect can lead to addictive behaviour or selfish behaviour around reward-seeking. Too much or too little can lead to a range of health issues including some mental health disorders.

Serotonin is another neurotransmitter, and some scientists also consider it a hormone. It occurs throughout the body and is used to send messages between nerve cells. Serotonin is a natural mood stabilizer and it may influence a range of physical and psychological functions including mood, emotions, appetite, and digestion. People with clinical depression often have low levels of serotonin. Serotonin is made from an amino acid called tryptophan. This is found in foods such as nuts, cheese, and red meat.

COMPONENTS OF A HAPPY LIFE

Sir Richard Layard, who has been researching happiness since the 1970s and is responsible for introducing the IAPT initiative in the NHS, has identified 7 areas of life which contribute to happiness:

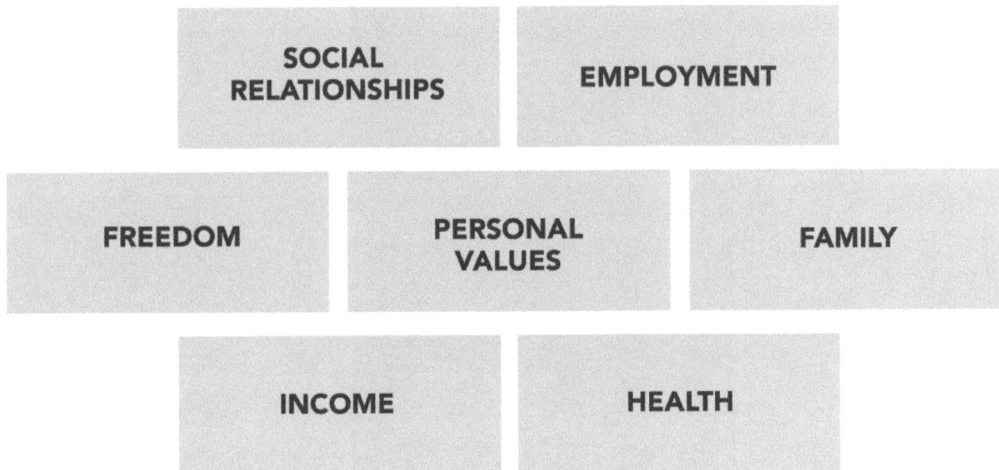

SOCIAL RELATIONSHIPS	EMPLOYMENT

FREEDOM	PERSONAL VALUES	FAMILY

INCOME	HEALTH

You may like to consider each of these in relation to your own life. If you can achieve a reasonable balance between all of them, you could expect to feel generally content. Clearly, some things are beyond our control (s*** happens!) but by prioritising your goals and putting effort into changing the things you can change, you can be responsible for many positive improvements in your life.

The message underlying all that we have said so far is that, to increase our levels of wellbeing, we need the 'four As':

- **Become AWARE of who we are now.**

- **ACCEPT what we can't change and ADDRESS what we can.**

- **ACT by taking responsibility for what we want to change.**

This brings us on to the next part of the book: **WHO DO I WANT TO BE?** In this part, we will explore how to accept what we have to accept, and how to make the changes to improve our lives.

Who Do I Want To Be?

~ PART TWO ~

Section 9

LEARNING TO ACCEPT

Accept yourself as you are, then decide to address what you *can* change
Within many of the areas that Professor Layard identified as contributing to our wellbeing, things will occur in your life that you can't change:

- Your **health** will be affected by illness, whether fleeting or chronic, and age.
- Your **employment** is subject to uncertainties such as the availability of the type of work you do, the requirements of employers, and the stability of the economic situation.
- Your **income** depends on several factors such as what your employer decides you are worth, and how promotion and career development are determined in your working world.
- Within your **family**, major life events such as birth and death are often in the hands of fate.
- In **social relationships**, other people's behaviour can influence how you feel.

(The remaining area, your **personal values** may be more open to examination and change). So, the first thing to say is that it helps to learn how to cope with these difficulties and challenges in the least damaging or upsetting way. This is to do with learning to be more realistic and **accepting**, which may involve:

- Understanding that we can change ourselves, but we can't change other people.
- Recognising that we need to learn to cope with difficulties and develop skills and qualities such as resilience and determination.
- Learning to think in a (realistically) positive or helpful way.
- Having realistic expectations.

- Being compassionate towards ourselves if we can't always achieve what we'd like or if we make mistakes.
- Learning to live in the present and not allowing our history and experience to overshadow our efforts to grow in the here-and-now.
- Behaving in ways that are likely to enhance and nourish relationships.
- Being prepared to take risks.
- Ensuring that we look after ourselves physically to ensure we are the fittest and healthiest we can be.

NATURE VS NURTURE

You can probably think of various things in your life as it is that can't be changed. Some of these are obvious, such as your height or your age, your position in your family of birth, and things that happened to you in the past.

How much are you influenced by your genes **(nature)** and how much by your environment **(nurture)**? This is a question that has fascinated philosophers for millennia. Research is advancing our understanding of the role of genetics in mental health. Scientists are researching the influence of our **genes** because this gives an insight into what causes behaviour; in other words, could your use of freewill be limited by the influence of your genetic predispositions? Certainly, some of us have talents or gifts that might not be available to everyone. However, the consensus seems to be that genes alone are unlikely to be responsible for a tendency towards behaviour, e.g., aggression. There is also little evidence currently (although research continues) that mental illness can be predicted by studying the genetic patterns within families. It is most likely that genes and environment interact to lead to particular behaviours.

Your **upbringing** and the **events** that occur during your life - particularly traumatic ones - can have a huge influence on how you navigate and respond to the world. For example, losing your job may make you unhappy, and you might feel like a failure; losing a loved one is almost certain to cause sadness and low mood, even leading to depression. It is now fairly widely accepted that if someone is brought up in a violent atmosphere or a dysfunctional family, they themselves will be likely to show antisocial tendencies in their own life. They may also develop certain triggers which fire the fight/flight response, often leading to defensive or aggressive behaviour; they may tend to have lower levels of serotonin.

The types of experience that are likely to manifest as **triggers** include:

- Rejection or abandonment – others might not want you, and your efforts towards connection are rebuffed; support is withdrawn.
- Exclusion – the feeling that you are left out while others seem to belong; you may even be laughed at or made fun of.
- Distrust – you might be betrayed or let down.
- Being subjected to physical harm.

We also need to consider **socio-economic factors** here; those who live in poverty and struggle to provide for the basic needs of themselves and their families are obviously likely to be at risk of greater stress.

Attachment theory focuses on the nurturing experiences of young children, hypothesising that the quality of the nurture offered by your primary caregivers can affect your ability to make relationships in later life.

Elements of your **culture** may also be relevant; language, religion and behaviour associated with your culture, and whether you are surrounded by people with a similar background, will affect your wellbeing.

Not all of these difficulties cause mental health problems as such; many of your reactions are simply natural, understandable responses to difficult experiences. However, recognising that you are under stress, unhappy or feeling low is nevertheless an important part of looking after yourself.

It is important as well to remember that what affects success in most things we want to do is our levels of **motivation**, **commitment,** and **perseverance**, which can be cultivated. While we can't, of course, anticipate events that may take place in the future, you might be surprised to find just how much can be improved by learning to adjust the way you respond to and think about what happens in your life.

"Whether you stay the same, or whether you change, this is **YOUR** choice. "

PREPARING FOR CHANGE

Remember, in many situations:

It is probably best just not to waste energy fighting the things we can't change. But as I try to show throughout the book, there is a great deal that you *can* change! Interestingly, we now know that the brain's neuroplasticity enables it to change its structure and function in significant ways. (A London taxi driver, who has memorised a mental map of the streets, has a noticeably large hippocampus!)

Learning to manage each aspect of experience in a healthy way will enable you to better tolerate things you find difficult, rather than trying to turn situations into what you want them to be. We will look at ways to do this in more detail in this second part of the book. It helps to group these aspects under particular headings (like those we saw on page 30) and then examine each of them in turn.

These are:

1. **PHYSICAL** (including health, exercise, diet, sleep)
2. **THOUGHTS** (expectations, rules and beliefs, negative versus positive, attitudes)
3. **BEHAVIOUR** (what you do when problems occur, how you make efforts to develop your strengths)
4. **EMOTIONS** (your feelings and how you manage them)

Section 10

IMPROVING OUR PHYSCIAL CONDTION

Please note – If you have any health worries or want well-informed advice, you should visit qualified health practitioners and websites belonging to reputable organisations. Although I have summarised some useful tips below, I am not a doctor and don't pretend to be a health expert; also, beware of those magical miracle cures you see advertised online! The best route to a healthy lifestyle is to adopt practices that can be built into your life long-term. For example, if you are trying to control your weight, crash diets are unlikely to bring about lasting change, but adopting a daily healthy eating pattern will be effective. Healthy living practices include:

General health:
- Take responsibility for looking after yourself.
- Do regular self-checks and ensure you carry out any checks suggested by your doctor.
- Keep up your dental checks.
- If you do have any long-term problems, see if you can find a support group locally.
- Make sure you have a healthy house: clean, but not full of harmful cleaning materials, furnished with supportive chairs, beds etc., well-lit, with windows that open to let in fresh air.
- Let yourself be cared for and ask for help when you need it.

Diet:
- Find out the nutritional value of what you eat, and which foods give the best value – lots of empty calories (as with sugar) don't help your health.

- Read the ingredients on food you're buying and try to avoid additives.
- Try to maintain a realistic nutritious diet. Some treats are fine but too many snacks can be harmful.
- Think about portion size: how much do you really need of each item on your plate?
- Make time for enjoying meals, and chew slowly (mindfully) so you really appreciate what you eat.
- Don't try do other things while you're eating (except socialising/talking).
- Take care with cooking (not too much fried food) and try to avoid processed food and too many takeaways.
- Choose food you enjoy - make food a pleasure.
- Monitor your caffeine, sugar and alcohol intake.

Sleep

- Make it a priority to ensure you develop healthy sleeping patterns.
- Notice the signs that tell you that you are getting short of sleep: you might be irritable, snappy, more stressed.
- Work out what is the optimum number of hours for you - we don't all need a fixed 8 hours.
- Look at your sleeping environment: is it quiet enough, dark enough, the right temperature?
- Try to stick to a regular routine if possible (parents of new babies excepted). Go to bed at a regular time and ensure that you wind down for sleep - stop screen time well beforehand, don't eat a big meal straight before bedtime, do things which make you naturally sleepy (have a warm bath or milky drink).
- Are you a lark or an owl? Your chosen bedtime and getting up time may be affected by this.

Exercise

- Become disciplined and make a definite decision to take regular exercise.
- This doesn't mean you must join a gym or start playing a sport; find out what's right for you (walking, dancing, swimming...) and allow yourself time to ensure you are able to participate.

The NHS recommends[4] that most able-bodied adults should do at least 150 minutes of moderate intensity activity a week or 75 minutes of vigorous intensity activity a week.

Relaxation

We'll come back to this later. There are all sorts of guides and techniques you can use to help yourself relax more. It really is important to reduce the stress in your life as much as you can, without resorting to drugs or addictive substances and behaviours.

You can see from reading this section that there are many changes you can make to improve and take care of your health. Yes, it may take some effort at first, and you're the one who decides how important it is to you. However, investing in your health now can only be good for you in the future and importantly, it will also improve your mental health and self-esteem!

Section 11

CHALLENGING THOUGHTS AND BELIEFS

On pages 19 – 28 we spent a lot of time exploring your beliefs, and I hope you began to see how much they influence your behaviour, your emotions, and your general wellbeing. You might have discovered that some of your thinking is unhelpful, and we're going to spend some time now looking at ways in which your underlying beliefs might be questioned – even adjusted – and how the thoughts that come into your head in different situations could be challenged for your responses – physical, behavioural and emotional – to be more conducive to a contented and enjoyable life.

Let's begin with those underlying beliefs and rules, and particularly your expectations – the *shoulds*, *oughts* and *musts*. Look back at those you identified on pages 21 and 22.

- How realistic are they?
- Does the evidence you have gained through your experiences in life support them?
- Are they very black and white?
- Do they involve a prediction or a condition about consequences (*'if…then…'*) and if so, have you found that the things you expect to happen actually do, in real-life examples?
- Do they involve making negative judgements about yourself?

These deep-seated beliefs are almost like **life scripts**, which are so deeply ingrained that you might not realise how much power they have over your day-to-day life.

To see how we can work to amend unhelpful beliefs, let's take an example; we'll explore the implications of belief **number 11** on page 22:

It is important that everyone should like me

This is the classic people pleaser's mantra. If you realise you are influenced by this belief, it may have originated during your upbringing, perhaps based on **'conditions of worth**' – something along the lines of, 'I will love you if…' (from parents) 'You will earn praise if…' (from school) or 'I will be your friend if…' These conditions would have encouraged you to behave in ways that other people wanted you to, and as a child, you would have enjoyed feeling accepted or cared about, so you would behave in the ways they wanted to gain these rewards.

An example might be the case of the small child who gets very angry when thwarted. The parent may tell him/her off and imply that the angry child won't be loved if (s)he behaves like that again. The child, experiencing confusion because (s)he wants to let people know how (s)he's feeling, fears losing the parent's love, so suppresses his/her anger and learns not to show it. Later in life, this pattern continues, so that the adult person, who is afraid of being rejected if (s)he expresses anger, lets other people treat him/her badly and doesn't protest.

You may not even have realised how anxious you are to please others. But let's look at the possible downside of being a people-pleaser:

- If you are taught that it's bad to make mistakes, you might become scared of not getting things 'right,' so you are reluctant to try new things or take on challenges.
- If you've learnt not to challenge authority, you might automatically accept criticism without questioning whether it is deserved or not.
- You might be scared of expressing certain feelings in case it upsets someone.
- You might get into trouble or do something you're uncomfortable with because you don't know how to say no.

- You might think of yourself as a failure if you don't live up to others' expectations.
- You might never put your own needs first, so end up feeling vaguely disappointed or unhappy a lot of the time without really knowing why.
- You are at risk of being exploited or taken advantage of by others.
- You may pass these unhelpful ideas on to your children.

You can probably think of more disadvantages to being a people-pleaser. Do spend time thinking about whether any of this applies to you. You really don't have to carry on like this! Furthermore, you are not responsible for other people's reactions! If someone doesn't like something you do or say, that is their problem, and while you might think carefully about a situation in which you find yourself at odds with someone else, you are under no obligation to change just to 'keep the peace' or please them.

Driven by deep-seated underlying beliefs which seem like rules for behaviour, people will be likely to show patterns of **unhelpful or distorted thinking**. Our thoughts are more accessible to us than those deeper beliefs, and in trying to help people with these kinds of problems, therapists will encourage clients to try to remember what they were thinking at the time a difficult or upsetting event took place. I'd like you to imagine you can look through a one-way mirror into my therapy room, where I am talking to 'Chris.'

Chris is a young man fresh out of university and about to start his new job. As a child, his parents were anxious that he should understand the value of hard work, which they said would lead to success. Even though he worked hard, they were quite critical of him and often seemed disappointed with him. He had few friends and would sometimes be teased by his peers for being a geek. Later this led to quite serious bullying. Today in his therapy session, we are exploring Chris's anxieties around starting work in an unfamiliar environment. In particular, he has fears about meeting his new colleagues.

Here is a snippet of our conversation: (Left = **T:** Therapist, Right = **C:** Chris)

T: "Chris, I understand that you are quite nervous about starting work next week. Tell me a bit about what you fear might happen when you meet these new people."

                              C: "I'm scared nobody will like me. I've always hated meeting new people."

T: "I notice you use the word 'nobody,' which feels like quite a big statement. What do you imagine they might be thinking when they meet you?"

                              C: "Well, they might look at me and think I'm weird. Maybe how I dress, or how I present myself in front of them."

T: "You imagine they might think you don't fit in. It seems you think they will make instant judgements, based on how you look."

                              C: "Yes, I've never really done the same things as other people. I never joined in groups at school."

T: "So, you feel as if you're different, and other people would think that too. What would that be like?"

                              C: "It would confirm that people don't like me. It doesn't matter how hard I've worked to get here, they'll spot that I'm an impostor, someone who doesn't belong."

T: "Can you explain what might happen if your thoughts were accurate?"

                              C: "I'd be rejected or laughed at. This would prove that I'm not good enough."

T: "That sounds very painful.
How might you behave in response to the situation?"

> **C:** "Mmm…I might pretend to be something I'm not
> to try to fit in. I would be thinking that if I can find a way of making them
> like me, things might be better."

T: "It's important you should be liked, and you would develop ways to
behave in order to try to appeal to them. What might this look like?"

> **C:** "I don't know…maybe I could try to be
> helpful by clearing up after the coffee break.
> Or try to make them laugh…or agree with things
> they say even if I don't really think they're right."

T: "You'd change to try to be accepted.
This sounds like quite a lot to ask of yourself.
I wonder if you can think of anything else that
might make life easier?"

> **C:** "Maybe I could try to avoid them –
> keep my head down and just get on with the job."

T: "While you are describing all this,
are there any voices from the past talking to you?"

> **C:** "Yes, my dad. He'd be telling me to 'man up' and get on with it. He
> would probably say I'm not trying hard enough and that I should be
> grateful to have the job."

Clearly, I have telescoped this conversation considerably, and in a real situation we would spend time in exploring each of these exchanges in much more detail, but for the sake of understanding the influence of unhelpful thinking, and the beliefs which underlie this, I'll pull out some examples of Chris's thoughts to examine in more depth.

1. *I'm scared nobody will like me. I've always hated meeting new people.*

Can you see how Chris has already made a **negative prediction** – so he is anticipating an unfriendly response from his new colleagues before he's even met them. The sad thing is, this may well become a self-fulfilling prophesy. He is likely to present as diffident and unsure of himself. Maybe he is exaggerating the imagined negativity ('*nobody*'…?), and it may be that he has a tendency to **catastrophise**.

2. …*they might look at me and think I'm weird. Maybe how I dress, or how I present myself in front of them.*

Chris seems to have the idea that he will be **judged**, and this will be based on his 'inadequate' appearance. There's a bit of **mindreading** going on here because he actually has no idea what they'll think: he has imagined their thoughts about him. He is also assuming they are the kind of people who attribute great importance to how people look.

3. *It would confirm that people don't like me. It doesn't matter how hard I've worked to get here, they'll spot that I'm an impostor, someone who doesn't belong.*

Here are some of Chris's negative beliefs about himself. These are more deeply ingrained than the more superficial thoughts and it will take some hard work to challenge them. I would work with Chris to seek **evidence** that people don't like him, and also perhaps challenge the idea that **everyone must like him**. The notion that he is an **impostor** is something which we find quite often, especially when people move up the career ladder – they find it hard to accept that they are good enough.

4. *I'd be rejected or laughed at. This would prove that I'm not good enough.*

Rejection – feeling unwanted or like an outsider is one of the most painful human experiences. (Think of solitary confinement as a punishment.) Very painful emotions accompany such experiences and in real-life therapy, we would spend a lot of time working to help Chris express his feelings and be listened to. Most therapists are guided by principles and attitudes which enable us to help people feel accepted and valued. As we are looking at thinking patterns here, I'll talk about these, but we will return to the emotional aspects later. One thing I hope our work would help Chris to realise is that his faulty thinking predisposes him to believe that he **deserves bad treatment,** and this is somehow down to his own inferiority. He **compares** himself to other people in a negative way and perhaps tends to **filter out** any evidence that contradicts this.

5. *I might pretend to be something I'm not to try to fit in. I would be thinking that if I can find a way of making them like me, things might be better.*

We can see an example of unhelpful behaviour here (trying to change what you do because you think others want you to), which we can come back to. However, what is significant is that Chris thinks he needs to change in order to please others. He has developed the idea that **love is conditional** upon him meeting certain requirements imposed by others. Again, a lot of work would be needed to unravel what has contributed to this, but I would certainly want to explore with Chris whether this strategy works and the possible drawbacks to behaving in a people-pleasing way. Note too, that he is taking full **responsibility** for the success of relationships and not factoring in the behaviour, preferences or wishes of others: they are also human beings who enter relationships for all sorts of reasons of their own. **Personalising** and making things all about you doesn't usually help us to see the bigger picture.

6. *…maybe I could try to be helpful by clearing up after the coffee break. Or try to make them laugh…or agree with things they say even if I don't really think they're right.*

This is a further example of people-pleasing but also demonstrates Chris' low self-esteem. He believes that if he can take on another persona or adopt a **false self** (because his real self isn't good enough), he will become more popular. The trouble with this is that he may experience negative outcomes because of his behaviour. Have you ever met the carer who is expected to be the family dogsbody or has turned into a martyr because (s)he resents not being appreciated? Have you seen people laugh behind someone's back because of their artificial-seeming mannerisms and behaviour? If someone plays the class clown, isn't (s)he likely to get into trouble? Worst of all, his/her integrity is challenged – (s)he is not **congruent** – and (s)he feels uncomfortable agreeing with things that actually compromise his/her values.

> 7. *Maybe I could try to avoid them – keep my head down and just get on with the job.*

This again shows unhelpful behaviour, and it links quite well with:

> 8. *…my dad. He'd be telling me to 'man up' and get on with it. He would probably say I'm not trying hard enough and that I should be grateful to have the job.*

This reminds Chris how, when he was younger, he was discouraged from showing feelings, and he learned to **suppress his emotions**. The problem with this is that all those pent-up feelings don't go away. You may remember how we talked about the effects of feelings on our bodies? Well, they also affect our thinking and our mental wellbeing. People who are exhorted to keep quiet/get over it/stop being a wuss etc. begin to **deny** that they have feelings, or they start to believe that there's something wrong with them if they feel pain, hurt etc. Another outcome could be the volcano effect: their squashed feelings build up to such an extent that they eventually explode (often true of angry feelings) and cause considerable damage to relationships.

This little vignette is imagined, but I hope it gives you some insight into the reasons it is important to learn more about the way you think and how this affects your life. If you are keen to explore this in more depth, start reading about CBT, or better still, find a therapist who can work with you. This can be transformative and help you to develop a healthy self-respect and sense of integrity. What might be useful here is to remind you of ways to challenge unhelpful thinking:

1. **Check for evidence** – has this actually happened/is it true or have I imagined it? Am I **mindreading**?

2. Is this a **fact or an opinion**? Would everyone see it the same way I do?

3. Ask: how appropriate is the **intensity** of my reaction to the event? How much will it matter in a week's time…a year from now?

4. Am I thinking in a **black-and-white** way? Is it possible the reality is somewhere in the middle? Are my '**rules**' interfering with the way I am understanding the situation?

5. Am I focusing only on the **negative**?

6. Identify: what actually disturbed me about this situation? Have I **personalised** it? Have I attached a meaning to it that isn't there? (e.g.: from memory) What 'button' is this pressing for me?

7. Explore: Is there **another way of seeing** this? What advice would I give someone else? How might someone else see this situation?

8. Imagine: What would be the **worst thing** that could happen?

Some therapists invite clients to record their thoughts over a period of time, to enable them to see where they might want to challenge unhelpful thinking and see if there are more helpful ways of understanding and responding to situations. This something you could try – then try challenging those thoughts!

Section 12

DEVELOPING HELPFUL BEHAVIOUR PATTERNS

On pages 37 and 38 we discussed different patterns of behaviour. I hope you are now more able to see when your behaviour in helpful, and when it isn't. In general, sulking, avoid difficulties, playing games, getting aggressive and blaming other people is not usually helpful. So, to enhance your wellbeing and your relationships, the first thing you need to do is:

START BY **ACCEPTING RESPONSIBILITY** FOR YOUR BEHAVIOUR.

Let's re-iterate - you can't make others behave the way you want them to. Yes, others may do or think things you don't like, they may misinterpret or misunderstand things that are going on, but you can't make them change. But you do hold responsibility for how you **react** to this, and you alone make the **choice** to behave the way you do as a consequence! Don't make excuses, and don't blame circumstances or other people. Find ways of reacting that leave you feeling good about yourself and free of the need to punish or hurt.

Learning Assertive Behaviour (pages 38 and 39) can help a great deal with this.

The best suggestion I can give at this point is that you practise being assertive as often as you can. I would start with fairly simple day-to-day situations, and this will equip you for dealing with bigger ones later.

Some general advice about being assertive, whether letting people know how you feel, or asking for something you want, is to prepare yourself. The following tips can be useful:

Be specific	Decide exactly what outcome you want, or precisely what you are feeling, and say so clearly and directly. Keep it simple and don't be tempted to go into reasons why you think it's someone else's 'fault.'
Be ready to repeat yourself	You may need to use the 'broken record' technique, where you repeat yourself as often as necessary, no matter what persuasion techniques others try to use on you. Don't get into arguments or justification.
Disclose your feelings	Accept that you may be nervous or anxious and share this; it will enable you to feel less need to defend yourself or suppress your emotions.
Use negative assertion	Especially when you are responding to criticism, learn to acknowledge the truth in what somebody says, but also be realistic about the degree of truth in the criticism.
Use negative enquiry	If someone has been critical of you, ask them to explain more about this. This will expose any manipulative criticism but enable you to learn from any that is constructive.
Maintain boundaries	Set limits on your own behaviour and on what you are prepared to tolerate from others or give to them. Be prepared to take a raincheck and walk away if necessary.
Know your rights	As a human being, you have a right to be treated with respect. You have a right to your feelings, views and opinions and to behave in accordance with these and to change them if you so please. (And so do other people!)
Aim for a reasonable compromise	This includes showing others that you have listened to them and have taken their views/feelings into account, but you also want your needs to be acknowledged and acted on.

Let's look at some examples of **situations that arouse strong reactions** and better ways to deal with them. We'll begin with some areas we looked at in part 1, pages 44-46: **dealing with conflict, saying no, asking for what you want, and handling criticism.** Remember that we are aiming for a win-win situation here: we are not seeking to put anyone down or score points or 'win' arguments! In general, you are likely to be more assertive if you are calm and clear-headed, so ensure you don't find yourself embroiled in trying to sort things out when you're emotionally highly charged. (The whole of section 13 is devoted to perhaps the most important aspect of improving your wellbeing: **expressing feelings**).

1. Dealing with conflict

When we feel under threat, as when we sense an impending conflict situation, we know that our reactions are likely to be either fight or flight. We need to look at these reactions now, because although they are natural responses, they can often result in harm being done. When we experience **stress** in our lives, the body releases several stress hormones, such as cortisol and adrenalin into the bloodstream. These hormones increase your concentration, ability to react, and strength. Also, your heart rate and blood pressure increase, and your immune system and memory are sharper. This is good if you have to deal with an urgent situation, and after you have dealt with the short-term stress, your body returns to normal.

However, problems can arise if you are under too much or chronic stress, and various health problems may result. Persistent adrenalin surges can damage blood vessels and arteries, increasing blood pressure and raising risk of heart attacks or strokes. Elevated cortisol levels create physiological changes that help to replenish the body's energy stores that are depleted during the stress response. But interestingly, they also contribute to the build-up of fat tissue and to weight gain: cortisol increases appetite, so that people will want to eat more to obtain extra energy; the stress response also increases storage of unused nutrients as fat. There are plenty of good reasons to try to lower your stress and reduce your reactions to it.

First, think about what you usually do in conflict situations. When you sense a conflict building, what is your usual reaction? How many of the following might apply to you?

HOW I BEHAVE	POSSIBLE UNDERLYING REASONS
I will take the blame for what's happened.	I prefer to keep the peace at all costs.
I will leave the room.	I am frightened by loud arguing.
I go quiet and refuse to discuss the issue.	I don't want to admit I'm wrong/to look foolish/to acknowledge a mistake.
I change the subject or try to soften the other person up.	I find it uncomfortable talking about negative feelings.
I criticise other people.	I want someone to blame.
I shout and get aggressive, even violent.	I get attention. It makes me feel powerful.
I list a whole lot of grievances.	I want to make the other person feel ashamed and convince them of my victimhood.
I try to provoke a fight.	I want to win/be proved right/get revenge/feel superior.
I endeavour to physically intimidate the other person.	If I can scare them, they might back down.

Continue to observe your own behaviour and find out how you react in different conflict situations. Your responses probably have a lot to do with those underlying beliefs we talked about above, (especially your *should/must/ought* beliefs), and the strength of your reactions will depend on emotional factors and triggers too. Work out whether your responses are helpful in delivering the outcomes you want or whether they just end up protracting the difficulty or leave you feeling more upset. You may identify patterns in your behaviour which come as if naturally to you, but which, when you look at them closely, are actually counterproductive. Fortunately, you can learn techniques to deal with conflict assertively and counter the stress response:

Negotiate rather than arguing

- Ensure that the time and place are right for talking the issue through. In the midst of a heated argument, it may be best to postpone further discussion to a later time. This will ensure you can focus on the subject in a calm way.

- Define the problem and ensure you both agree with this definition. Make sure each person gets the chance to put the situation as they see it. Then you can understand where the differences lie. When it's your turn to listen, make sure you do. It helps to summarise both points-of-view before moving on and to show empathy for others' feelings.

- Acknowledge and respect differences. This is often one of the hardest things to do. People want to feel that they are right, and no other point-of-view can co-exist! But many situations simply aren't that black-and-white. Some people like their music loud, others can't stand noise; some people think kids should be punished if they misbehave, others prefer to discuss and explain…and so on. This could be the most valuable part of the talk because you really begin to understand each other's views and feelings.

- Think of all the possible solutions you can - even bizarre ones! Though each of you may have a clear idea of what they would like the outcome to be, it is important to see what other potential answers there may be.

- Evaluate each possible solution, from both sides, looking for room to negotiate, compromise or agree limits.

- Choose a solution that is acceptable to both of you. It is important that you remember that this isn't about winning. Don't just try to bully the other person round to what you want. You may need to make concessions, and then it would be reasonable to expect them to do the same. This is the art of negotiation! What we are looking for is the win-win situation.

- Try solutions out and evaluate your success. Agree what you are going to do and give yourselves a period of time during which you will stick to this; come back later to see how it worked. Keep the topic open and be willing to make adjustments.

Throughout this process, remember: If things get tricky: relax, take time out, come back when you feel better. At no point should either party make personal or critical remarks about the other, but should try to use 'I' statements, owning their feelings and views.

2. Saying no

One of the reasons people don't like saying no is because they don't want other people to think they're selfish. However, putting other people before ourselves in this way can mean we spend an awful lot of time doing things we don't want to, with people we don't want to be with. So, the outcome of never saying no can be that we become unable to recognise, express or meet our own needs, and we may also make ourselves miserable in the process. When we talk about becoming assertive, we are taking account of the needs of ourselves as well as others. No-one is saying we should approach situations from a purely selfish point-of-view all the time. What is important is that we should, in considering requests made to us, be able to weigh up thoughtfully and considerately, how the situation feels from the viewpoint of everyone involved – and that includes ourselves.

Example:

Let's go back to Chris. He happened to mention earlier in the day that he wasn't doing anything that evening. That's not quite true, because he had a box set lined up and he wanted to ring a mate for a chat. He was looking forward to a nice relaxing evening. Then a colleague (Rick) came up to him:

**"Oh, hi Chris, glad I caught you.
Listen, mate, my wife's mum has just phoned and asked her to go
round, but I'd already arranged to go to the darts match.
You couldn't babysit the kids again, could you?"**

Chris's heart sinks. Rick has done this before and though Chris's internal bully is telling him he should do this, otherwise Rick won't think much of him, Chris can already feel himself getting nervous; he finds the children hard to control and feels a bit resentful that Rick didn't even leave him anything to eat or drink last time. Underneath, he knows he wants to say no.

As his therapist, I might work with him like this:

T: "Chris, try to state out loud how you feel about this situation, and how you would actually like to respond."

C: "Well, to tell the truth, I feel a bit resentful. Rick doesn't ever return the favour, and he's dropped things on me at the last minute before. It's not as if his darts is essential. But then, I'm not doing anything important either. I'd want to refuse. But I'd find this really difficult."

T: "I wonder if you feel a bit underappreciated. It seems as if you don't feel Rick treats you very respectfully."

C: "It is a bit as if he uses me."

T: "Can you explain why you'd find it difficult to refuse?"

C: "I don't really know how to do it. If I said I'm already busy, I'd know I wasn't really telling the truth. If I said I didn't want to, he might be offended. If I dithered, I think he'd just go on at me. I don't want to fall out with him."

T: "I wonder if you're worried about what he might think of you; perhaps you feel he might dislike you or reject you?"

C: "Yes. It would be awful if that happened.

I couldn't stand being disliked."

T: "This is something we've talked about a lot. The idea that you might be disliked, and this would be awful, and it would all be your responsibility. Let's break some of this down a bit. Can you identify any unhelpful beliefs or thoughts here? What about the idea that you should always tell the truth? Can you see that you may not be telling the truth to *yourself* – i.e.: that your nice relaxing evening doesn't matter? The plan you had made for yourself *did* mean that you were already busy!"

C: "But wouldn't that mean I was being selfish?
I was always taught that this is wrong."

T: "What do you think about this now?
Is it selfish to take care of yourself
by making sure you get to relax?
As to Rick's being 'offended'
– what does this mean?"

C: "Well, he may think I don't like babysitting for his kids."

T: "And if he does… whose problem is that?
Let's just look at the last thing you said:
'I don't want to fall out with him.'
Can you spot any unhelpful thinking here?"

C: "I suppose I may be mindreading –
I don't know what he'd think or how he'd react.
Mmm… and I may be catastrophising
– he probably wouldn't completely reject me.
He might be a bit miffed if he has to miss his darts,
but that's not my fault. It was his wife who let him down."

T: "So, can you sum up how you're feeling now?"

C: "I still want to say no, and though I realise

> I don't like doing it, I feel more confident about the idea.
> After all, I'm not responsible for his problems
> and how he feels."

T: "Well done!
Perhaps you can practise the things
we've talked about here,
so that you're better prepared for next time."

It's a real skill to be clear about how much you are prepared to offer in particular circumstances. In many cases, this is about **boundaries** and setting limits. While most of us probably like to be flexible, there are limits to what we tolerate and points at which we begin to feel we are being taken advantage of.

Look at the chart on the following page, which shows step-by-step how to deal with requests from other people.

RESPONDING TO REQUESTS

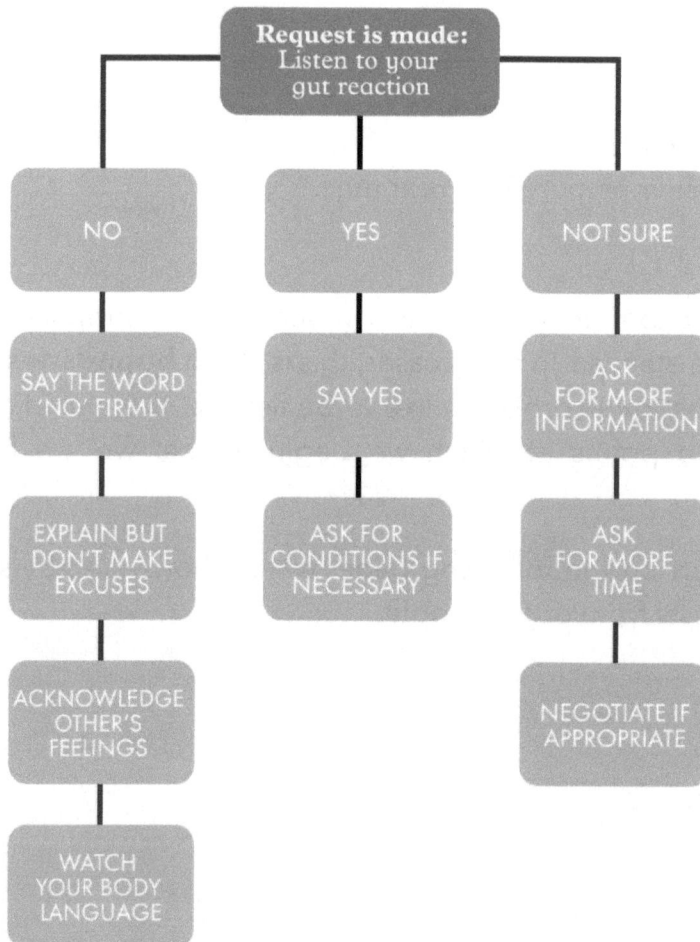

```
                    ┌──────────────────────┐
                    │  Request is made:    │
          ┌─────────┤  Listen to your      ├─────────┐
          │         │  gut reaction        │         │
          │         └──────────┬───────────┘         │
    ┌─────┴─────┐      ┌────────┴────────┐     ┌──────┴──────┐
    │    NO     │      │      YES        │     │  NOT SURE   │
    └─────┬─────┘      └────────┬────────┘     └──────┬──────┘
    ┌─────┴─────┐      ┌────────┴────────┐     ┌──────┴──────┐
    │SAY THE WORD│     │    SAY YES      │     │    ASK      │
    │ 'NO' FIRMLY│     │                 │     │ FOR MORE    │
    └─────┬─────┘      └────────┬────────┘     │ INFORMATION │
    ┌─────┴─────┐      ┌────────┴────────┐     └──────┬──────┘
    │EXPLAIN BUT │     │   ASK FOR       │     ┌──────┴──────┐
    │DON'T MAKE  │     │ CONDITIONS IF   │     │    ASK      │
    │EXCUSES     │     │ NECESSARY       │     │ FOR MORE    │
    └─────┬─────┘      └─────────────────┘     │   TIME      │
    ┌─────┴─────┐                              └──────┬──────┘
    │ACKNOWLEDGE │                             ┌──────┴──────┐
    │OTHER'S     │                             │NEGOTIATE IF │
    │FEELINGS    │                             │APPROPRIATE  │
    └─────┬─────┘                              └─────────────┘
    ┌─────┴─────┐
    │WATCH      │
    │YOUR BODY  │
    │LANGUAGE   │
    └───────────┘
```

There are various types of 'no' that you could use, depending on the outcome you want.

- Straight no – with no apology: brief, direct but doesn't have to be abrupt – aim for polite, calm, firm.
- Thoughtful no – acknowledging the other's viewpoint, but still saying no.
- Rational no – explaining why (but note: this may give 'ammunition' to someone who wants to argue with you).
- Time-out no – postponing e.g.: *'I'd like some time to think about that first.'*

- Enquiring no - asking if the person would accept some other arrangement.
- Broken record no - repeated for persistent people.

One type of 'no' is *not* to be recommended:
- Indirect no - you say yes then you show people through sulks or other behaviour that you don't really feel happy about agreeing; this isn't being authentic and could be experienced as manipulative.

Of course, sometimes you will want to take into account other aspects of the situation, which is when you might use the 'time-out' no and ask for more information or more time. I find it really helpful in many circumstances to say to someone *'I'll have a think about it and get back to you.'* You might then be able to consider whether this relationship is reciprocal in any way - e.g.: does Rick do anything to help Chris at times? He could consider asking for a favour in return.

Receiving a 'no'

It can feel uncomfortable when people refuse us. But remember their rights are the same as ours. If a request you make gets a refusal, see whether there are any alternatives; would you be prepared to settle for less? Is it worth persisting or is it better to accept this without feeling it as a personal rejection?

ASKING FOR WHAT YOU WANT

Remember: we all have a right to express our needs and ask for what we want; by being able to do this, we can build up our self-respect. However, we don't automatically have the right to *get* what we want. When making requests, these tips may help you:

1. Know exactly what you want, and don't be influenced by what you think you 'ought' to want.
2. Be specific, and try to phrase things positively (not: *'don't do that here'*, but *'please will you do that in the kitchen'*).
3. Don't pretend that something is OK if it's not - your feelings are probably showing, so it's best to be open and not avoid saying what you want.

4. Always use 'I' rather than generalising or de-personalising ('*I would prefer to…*' rather than '*it would be better if…*') and avoid criticising someone else.

5. Be direct: don't drop hints/expect people to guess what you want/become manipulative to try to get your own way.

6. Respect the other person's point-of-view and let them know you have heard them.

7. Accept differences: For example, I am not a person who talks for long on the phone – I use it for specific purposes and try to keep conversations short; therefore, if someone rings me up for no particular reason other than to chat, I am apt to feel irritated. I have now learnt to make it clear at the start of the conversation how long I've got: '*Oh hi, Mandy. Lovely to hear from you, but I'm afraid I've only got about twenty minutes.*' (Then stick to it!)

Over big issues, it may be best to prepare carefully: arrange a time which is mutually convenient to discuss the subject; prepare what you want to say, bearing in mind the need to be respectful; be clear about your desired outcome/how far you are prepared to negotiate. It is easy to get side-tracked and other people may become defensive, but make sure you stick to the subject. Always remember, this is not a point-scoring exercise, and it's not about who 'wins': ideally, you want a satisfactory outcome for both parties.

HANDLING CRITICISM
When you're on the receiving end:
To help you respond more assertively to criticism, try to get into the habit of going through each of the following 4 stages:

- **Listen** to the criticism and think about it rather than reacting immediately, even if you feel a strong emotional reaction; ask for clarification if you don't understand anything.
- **Decide** if it's fair or accurate – or partly so (this may be quite painful and may even be the most important part of the process).
- **Respond** – you have a variety of responses available to you depending on the level to which you agree with the criticism *(see below).*
- **Let it go** once it's been dealt with, don't store it away to erode your self-esteem; similarly, don't save up your anger for an argument later.

- **Make any necessary changes** and **learn any lessons** from the situation; often mistakes are our best way of learning - treat them as important learning opportunities.

When choosing your response, the following can be helpful:

If the criticism is true or fair:
Accept it but don't beat yourself up with guilt or shame; perhaps ask for help in putting the situation right:
'You're right, I didn't do that very carefully. I'll try to sort it out. Thanks for letting me know.'

If it's only partly true:
Accept the true part, but clarify the exaggerated /untrue bit:
'Yes, I know I was a bit careless today. But this doesn't often happen.'
Ask them for clarification:
'I don't understand. Could you explain that?'

If it's wholly untrue:
Make a clear rejection of the criticism, adding something more affirming if appropriate:
'No. I don't agree. I'm not a lazy person - this was unusual for me.'

If it's a deliberate put-down:
Don't be made to feel bad - just calmly acknowledge any truth in the criticism, but add your own view of the situation:
'Yes, you're probably right. This hasn't been my best day.'

If the person is having a go at you in general, it sometimes helps to use **fogging**. This means you agree with anything that clearly is true but refuse to be put down by anything else, or to enter a discussion about the content of the criticism. If the person wants you to feel bad, you need to show them that you don't. For example, your mum might be having a real go at you, listing a lot of faults:

'You never tidy up your room...you just don't seem to care about anything...you're a complete mess....'

When you can get a word in, you just say quietly, briefly and calmly:
'Yes, you're probably right, I am sometimes untidy,' and get on with what you're doing.

Giving Criticism

Situations sometimes arise in which we have to give criticism to someone else. This can often happen at work. By sticking to a few simple rules, and following certain steps, we can make this relatively painless for both parties.

Remember, if you are too *passive* and you wrap the criticism up in a lot of waffle, the person may not get the message, or won't take it seriously; if you say nothing, they either won't be aware of the problem, or they'll happily ignore it. If you are *aggressive*, things could escalate to a row with unpleasant personal remarks being made. *Manipulative* behaviour is sometimes used in situations like this (*'If you carry on like that, you'll make me ill'*) – which often results in guilt or distancing between people. To give criticism *assertively*, take these steps:

1. Clarify the problem

Make sure you are in a calm frame of mind. Clarify what you want to focus on and don't get into generalisations about the person as a whole. If you can see the situation as a problem that needs solving, rather than a battle to be fought, it may help. Be clear what has to change but also acknowledge good points.

Shirley, the supervisor, realises that recently she frequently has had to find cover for Stan first thing in the morning because he isn't there. When she observes the situation closely, she finds that he is at least 15 minutes late most days. He needs to arrive on time.

2. Take the conversation seriously

Choose a suitable time and place to talk, ensuring there is sufficient privacy.

Shirley asks Stan to come to her office at an agreed time.

3. State your grievance clearly

Don't get side-tracked. Make a clear statement of the problem as you see it and be specific about any criticism. Try not to make personal comments or evaluations, but stick to facts.

Shirley says: 'Stan, you are usually punctual, but you have been arriving about 15 minutes late for several days now. It has been difficult for everyone to cover for you until you arrive.'

4. Describe your feelings

Calmly express your feelings about the behaviour you are concerned about, choosing your words carefully and accurately.

'I find myself getting more annoyed each time this happens because it makes more work for me and takes me away from what I'm meant to be doing'.

5. Listen to the other person

Give the other person a chance to respond to this, being careful not to let yourself get side-tracked into talking about their problems.

Shirley: 'Can you explain why this is happening?
Stan explains that his wife has a new job, and he must take their son to school now. This is causing him to be late.

6. Show empathy but stick to your point

Shirley responds that she understands that childcare can be difficult. However, she reminds him that according to his contract he is responsible for working from 9 o'clock. Shirley repeats that she would like to see Stan at 9 each day.

7. Brainstorm possible solutions

How could the situation be improved? It may be possible to find a solution that suits you both. Think together of as many different ways of solving the problem as you can.

Shirley asks what possible solutions there may be to this problem. He and his wife may need to consider their childcare arrangements. Shirley and Stan think of a number of things, including looking into whether Stan could arrange to share the school run; whether the children could attend breakfast club etc. If there is still a problem, he may need to talk to the manager.

8. Find the best solution and agree the changes that will take place.

Shirley and Stan agree about what might be worth trying and clarify his responsibilities. In the meantime, he must arrive on time.

9. Agree a further meeting to discuss progress.

BEHAVOURIAL TECHNIQUES

As well as learning to be assertive, there are of course many other behaviours which will encourage good mental health and wellbeing. One thing that is vital is to ensure that you take time out to really **relax**. There are all sorts of ways you can learn to relax, but you need to prioritise this as part of your wellbeing practice. There isn't time to go into all the different forms of relaxation in detail here, but I'll summarise some of the ways that are available and then you might want to look up websites, podcasts, apps etc which make use of these methods.

1. Relaxed breathing

You can develop ways of calming your breathing so that it feels gentle and regular. If you want a quick exercise which you can do anywhere, anytime:

Stop what you're doing, relax your shoulders and take a deep, slow breath in and hold it for 5 seconds. Allow your abdomen to expand as you do this. Breathe out slowly and steadily, keeping the outbreath going as long as you can, to ensure your lungs really empty. Relax before you inhale again. Repeat this several times.

Some people find that imagining they are breathing in the colour blue, and breathing out the colour red can enhance this experience.

2. Progressive muscle relaxation (spend about 15-20 minutes on this)

Relax one muscle group at a time until your whole body is in a state of relaxation. (There are lots of audio recordings to help with this). This is useful to help you get to sleep as well.

Sit or lie somewhere comfortable and quiet. Begin to focus on the sensations around you and breathe calmly, releasing any tension you notice.

Gradually scan each part of your body, noticing any tension and letting it go. (I often experience a sense of parts of my body dropping or flopping as I do this!)

Work from your head, through your neck, then your arms and hands - almost as if you are letting your arms go limp.

Next to your back, neck to hips. You may feel as if you are sinking down into a chair. (Again, find your own way of doing this; I sometimes lie on the bed and imagine it's a sort of blancmange or modelling clay and I am moulding my shape into it).

Let your legs and feet move naturally as you release the tension from them – perhaps they will roll outwards.

Return to your breathing…it may be getting slower and deeper as you become more relaxed.

When you are ready to stop, don't rush this; open your eyes, then gradually start with little movements – e.g.: wiggling your fingers and toes. Have a good stretch. Rise slowly.

3. Learn mindfulness

It really helps to research this one! Maybe join a group where mindfulness is taught. I can only give a superficial summary here.

Mindfulness means being very much in the present moment, paying attention in a focused, purposeful way, without any judgement. You will learn to notice physical sensations, sights, sounds and smells – things which you normally might not notice. Just let any thoughts go – don't dwell on them.

(I have never forgotten, years ago, when my beloved nephew was very little, a christening party was held for him in the garden. I was bringing him down the path to talk to everyone and he stopped, bent down, and picked up a tiny snail on the end of his finger. He squatted on his haunches and became totally engrossed watching it, as if at that moment, there was nothing else in the world. That's what I call mindfulness!)

I recommend going for a walk in a mindful way, especially in the country or at the seaside:

Try to ignore any thoughts that come into your head and stay in the here-and-now.

Listen – to the crunch of your footsteps, the sounds of birds (and believe me, the more you tune in, the more you'll appreciate what a huge variety there is!) or the crashing of waves…Or stand very still and enjoy the silence.

Touch – textures of bark, moss, pebbles etc. Feel the breeze in your hair.

Smell – salt in the seaside air, perfumes within the flowers, the peaty soil of the woodland.

Watch, and really see - the tiniest movement can indicate some kind of life, whether it's an insect, a bird or a mammal. Follow the racing squirrel in a tree or the circling buzzard high in the sky; look at cloud patterns, colours… go out at night and see what's there.

Taste – the salt in the air, the rain or snow, a freshly picked blackberry.

It's easy to take so much for granted, but it's experiences like this that foster contentment. (Another of my stories: my granny, in a wheelchair for many years, had been living in a care home for a long time and hardly ever went out. One day, I was appalled when I arrived, to see her sitting by an open window, getting wet. I rushed over to close it, but she cried out, *'No, please don't! I haven't felt the rain on my face for 16 years!'*)

4. Use visualisation and imagery

It is often the case that it helps to think of something positive if you are experiencing a low mood. By thinking of something positive you are more likely to feel calm and relaxed. You may find, when you have done one of the relaxation exercises, it is enjoyable to extend this into a guided imagery visualisation. This is something which, if you practise enough, can easily be summoned when you are in distress. A lot of people refer to it as their '**safe place.**' Once you are in a relaxed state, this is how you start:

Think of a place you find comforting, or where you can remember feeling happy. A lot of people choose somewhere they have been on holiday, or a happy memory from earlier in their lives. Close your eyes and spend a few minutes imagining this place in as much detail as you can; don't rush this – really focus.

- Concentrate on what you can see, even down to the smallest details.
- Listen to all the sounds around you, both near and distant.
- If you are eating or drinking or just breathing some beautiful fresh air, be aware of the atmosphere and the scents and tastes.
- What physical sensations are you aware of? What can you feel? What is the temperature like? Soak up the sensation of anything you can touch.
- Be aware of what is happening in each part of your body.

When you have done this a few times, you can take this further by attaching a key phrase to it and repeating this to yourself. For example, one of my safe places is a beautiful sea in Croatia where I am snorkelling among glorious fish. When I use the word 'snorkelling,' because I have practised this so much, many of the pleasant, carefree feelings associated with this experience are brought into my mind. I can use this anywhere, anytime, simply by closing my eyes and repeating the word and it helps to calm me down.

You probably won't find that you take to all these relaxation activities, but there may be one that you can practise and become sufficiently good at, so that you have a strategy for helping you during stressful times.

Of course, relaxation isn't just about becoming very peaceful. Plenty of other ways of choosing to spend time can be beneficial.

There are lots of other things you can do to enhance your sense of wellbeing. Helpful activities tend to fall into three overlapping categories:

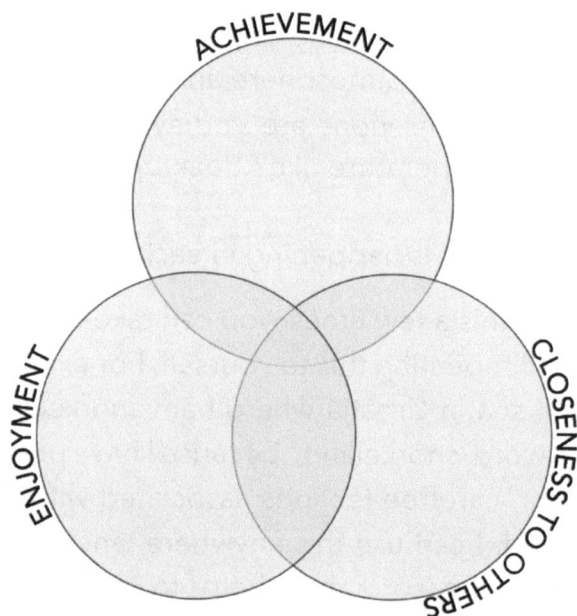

ACHIEVEMENT

ENJOYMENT

CLOSENESS TO OTHERS

RELATIONSHIPS

You will remember that Professor Layard (page 65) highlighted the importance of social relationships and friends. Much importance is attached, in writing about wellbeing, to the establishment of social and emotional bonds. (But this applies to meaningful relationships – not 'friends' on social media!) People who enjoy **close relationships** with family and friends receive emotional support that indirectly helps to sustain them at times of stress and crisis. The neurological and physiological basis for this has been researched in recent years, particularly that which looks into the role of the **vagus nerve**, which communicates between the main organs and the brain, so that we can see how physical health and positive emotions are linked. Being socially connected fosters positive emotions and thereby contributes to good health.

Closeness to one individual in particular is of course also life-enhancing and gets the dopamine flowing! But we must never assume that this is easy or take it for granted. Commitment involves a long-term process of learning and being flexible and open to change, and even then, there are no guarantees of long-term satisfaction. Many myths about love feed the notion that everlasting love involves some kind of magic. It doesn't. It's bloody hard work!

There are, however, lots of things you can do to develop and improve a sense of closeness and it is worth exploring how much you contribute towards making your close relationships as pleasurable as you can. How many of these do you do on a regular basis?

- Give a kiss or hug when you say goodbye.
- Organise little treats for the person you love.
- Show interest in your partner's day and really listen when (s)he talks about it.
- Pay your partner compliments.
- Behave in a demonstrative, affectionate way.
- Look after someone when they feel tired or down.
- Make time to be together and have fun.
- Help and contribute to looking after the house/children/pets etc.
- Tell people what you love about them.
- Share plans and dreams.
- Confront difficulties in a constructive way.

So much could be said about building healthy relationships that it would make at least one more book in itself. The point is, we mustn't get complacent or fail to nurture our precious relationships.

It is also important to build **new relationships**. One thing I have often noticed is that some people, especially if they're a bit shy, find all sorts of 'reasons' for not making the first gesture towards friendship, expecting others to come to them. (Years ago, a lonely friend of mine who hadn't had a boyfriend for ages, was sitting in her front room when suddenly a passing gang of football supporters literally threw their mate through her window into the room. But this is exceptional!) Usually, someone must take responsibility for getting to know another person. It may be risky to offer an invitation or suggest an outing, but someone must be the first, and once you've learnt to challenge any unhelpful thoughts around rejection, why shouldn't this be you?

The key to growing your social network is to plan to do this and then stick to it – but don't be too ambitious to start with. Achieving small goals can help you to gain the confidence to try more – for instance, one suggestion might be to promise yourself to attend a new event every month, or to initiate at least one conversation every day. For example, you could:

- Start by contacting a friend you haven't seen for a long time.
- Say good morning to a stranger.
- Pay a compliment to someone you meet – shop assistant, fellow-traveller, passer-by.
- Start chatting to the next person in a queue.
- Talk to a dog-walker by making friends with their pet.

Another incident I remember happened on a training day. The tutor gave us all 6 penny pieces and told us to go out into the town (which was unfamiliar to most of us) and give each one to a total stranger. We were all a bit taken aback and anxious at first, anticipating hostile reactions. But every single person had positive, and mainly humorous, experiences, and no-one brought any pennies back with them! When we overcame our initial fears, we had fun!

Connecting with people isn't just about your close family: many people get a great deal of satisfaction from contributing to their community, either by volunteering or by sharing their skills and talents and joining like-minded groups of people. Think about the last time you did something kind or generous for a stranger. How did it make you feel? Being generous towards others and giving in general enhances our wellbeing more than acquiring material improvements for ourselves. I have a lot more to say about this on page 129.

I'd like to make a final point here: I strongly feel that it is not only people we feel close to - the value of a pet, or connections to animals has been shown to be tremendously rewarding, and pet therapy is now quite a regular form of support for people with difficulties or who are lonely. Have you considered this as a way to improve your mental wellbeing? If you can't have a pet yourself, could you consider volunteering at an animal charity, or walking someone's dogs?

ACHIEVEMENTS

These come in lots of forms: making things, doing work on your home, learning something new, gaining new skills, raising a family and so on. Whether at work or at leisure, there are lots of things we can do to boost our sense of achievement and success. However, it sometimes feels really difficult to get started and lethargy sets in. Our mindset is relevant here. In general, developing a **positive mindset** is likely to involve some or all of the following:

- A clear recognition of your own skills, strengths and qualities (some as yet only potential).
- An understanding that achievement involves challenge, effort, some setbacks, and a time commitment.
- A belief that any rewards are for your own growth and satisfaction and not about how others might judge you.
- Knowing that you don't have to be great at something to enjoy it.
- Giving up perfectionism while striving to be the best you can.
- Believing that mistakes can be points of learning.
- Remembering that an interest in something can lead to an ability to do it well - some of your talents are still undiscovered!

Let's take the areas of work and leisure separately, and see what we could do in each arena.

Achievement at work

Whether we think about paid work, voluntary work or work at home, it is worth looking at what you consider to be success and pleasure in these areas. This is not necessarily about gaining financially or getting qualifications, but more about using your potential. Take a look at what work is like for you by asking any of the following questions which might be relevant:

1. Does the work take up an amount of time that you are comfortable with?
2. At work, do you feel sufficiently challenged?
3. Do you feel there is enough opportunity for growth, promotion, or development?
4. Are the rewards (financial or otherwise) good enough and do you feel you are valued?
5. Do you enjoy the contact you have with others?
6. Is the journey to work reasonable?
7. Are others factors satisfactory – holidays, healthcare, pension rights etc?
8. What gives you the most/least satisfaction about the work?

There may be ways you could get more satisfaction, even from a job you enjoy. Think about whether:

1. You could improve your performance – e.g.: through training, asking for more responsibility, learning to delegate etc.
2. There are ways you might work better within your team – by sharing responsibilities more clearly, getting to know each other better, carrying out appraisals and planning professional development.
3. You could examine how resources are used.

If you want to plan your career over the next few years, take steps to do this now by developing your skills and looking out for learning opportunities. Some people find it helps to create goals. We'll talk about this in the third part of the book. As you progress, it's important to notice and acknowledge your achievements, however small.

Enjoyment: your leisure time

How do you spend your leisure hours and is this providing a satisfactory balance? Who do you spend them with – do you see enough of the people you care about? If it helps, draw pie charts of how things are, then how you'd like them to be, so you can set about deciding how to change what you need to (see page 61).

Join a club or resign from a committee; re-set your standards if you are a perfectionist so you don't have to do everything to the optimum level; enlist help e.g.: from family members to deal with chores; give up things that have ceased to interest you and look at notice boards etc. to see what's going on in your area.

While connecting with others is an important element of wellbeing, some forms of pleasure involve getting engaged with solitary pastimes such as reading or painting, which give you a sense of creativity and achievement too. There are thousands of things you could potentially do; you may have hobbies or interests which have perhaps been neglected - music, photography, writing, sport and so on, or you may want to investigate new ideas which are offered on courses or workshops. Sometimes enjoyment is just about expressing yourself: dancing, playing an instrument - banging a drum if you're so inclined!

Experiment: curiosity can spawn all kinds of new ideas and sometimes we have been so limited by past experience that we don't realise how much exciting stuff there is out there in the world! You may have been offered a fairly narrow curriculum at school, but colleges now offer training in all sorts of things from dog grooming to beauty therapy to psychology. Find out what piques your interest! (My mid-life career change to counselling grew from attending an adult evening class).

Can you see how all these helpful activities can link together to help you gain more meaning in your life and increase your motivation and satisfaction?

While it is always important to be realistic (most of us will never be opera singers or world tennis champions) it is also true to say that none of these improvements will happen without:

You are responsible for making changes; you need to develop attitudes and thought patterns that are positive, and you need to be committed to achieving your goals. (They say it took Thomas Edison 1000 attempts at making an electric light bulb work; he didn't give up, even at attempt number 999!) All this is discussed in Part three, page 143, but remember, we are

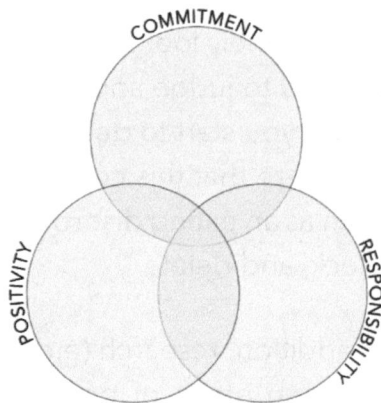

currently trying to answer the question 'Who do I want to be?' and I hope you are beginning to get a sense of ways you might develop and expand your life to enhance your level of contentment and wellbeing.

SOCIAL MEDIA AND MENTAL HEALTH

While we're talking about behaviour, it's worth considering your online behaviour, especially in respect of social media. People these days pay enormous attention to the reactions they get on Facebook, Instagram etc. but this isn't always good for their mental wellbeing.

For example, you may achieve little 'hits' of dopamine through receiving lots of likes etc., so you start to seek more and more. This is like an addiction, so that you may feel almost as if you can't help it. The more you do this, the less you do other things, and ultimately you may lose the motivation to do work or other important activities. We like to think that by using these online sites we are connecting to the world; I would ask – when did you last speak to a stranger?

Your self-esteem is very likely to be affected if you read negative stuff about yourself; if you feel worse after reading a comment, then it's best to avoid that comment section or that person. The long-term effect of reading any negative stuff about yourself (even from totally unknown people) could be depression and anxiety. A particularly sensitive area for many people is around their looks and this is something which some people seem to feel entitled to judge and comment on, on social media, even if they don't know you. If you start to develop distorted thoughts about your body, you need to be aware that this could ultimately lead to serious mental health conditions such as an eating disorder or body dysmorphia. It's OK to unfriend, unfollow, block, and delete.

In addition, research (e.g.: work by Antonio Damasio[5]) is beginning to show that one effect of preoccupation with social media can be to lessen our capacity to understand the emotions of others and to empathise. This might mean you become less able to nurture healthy long-term relationships. We pick up so much from being with people that you could miss out on important signals from body language, tone of voice, facial expressions etc. and get less skilled at reading these when you are with someone.

Furthermore, reading things that only require a short attention span could leave you less able to read longer stuff such as books, which ultimately compromises your learning and development. Concentration and attention are vital to processing information.

Things you might consider doing in order not to get trapped into negative addictive behaviour patterns around social media include:

- Limiting your time on social media; it may be worth monitoring how much time you spend on various sites and why: what do you get out of this? The paradox of 'Fear Of Missing Out' is that while you're so busy looking at what everyone else is doing, you're not actually doing anything yourself!

- Choose platforms where anonymity is not possible (people tend to censor themselves less when they can be anonymous - and remember, many of them probably don't know you!)

- Avoid reading negative comments. You may have to be firm about limiting the amount you read and deciding whether responding to comments is helpful or damaging to you.

- Stay firm in your values: don't allow yourself to be swayed by what other people think; be clear about your beliefs around what is acceptable and behave in ways that you feel to be right.

- Give significance to positive comments and the support of friends who really know you, and get into the habit of posting positive comments yourself.

Section 13

WORKING WITH EMOTIONS

As I said before, emotions are natural and you need to be able to feel, recognise and express a range of emotions, but extremes of emotion can cause problems. Many people experiencing long-term powerful emotional reactions tend to behave in ways that aren't helpful, such as:

- Using substances/alcohol
- Self-harm
- Unhelpful eating patterns
- Difficulty managing anger

This can in turn lead us to feel worse about ourselves, setting up a vicious cycle. We need to learn and practise helpful coping strategies in order to overcome this.

While saying that you are responsible for regulating your feelings, I'm not suggesting that they don't matter or that you should try to discourage them; emotions are extremely important in influencing your wellbeing! However, how you deal with them is critical to your physical and mental health. This section looks at better ways of responding to emotion.

EXPRESSING FEELINGS

I hope that during the first part of this book, you started to become more aware of your feelings and more able to be specific in naming them precisely. Now it's time to think about ways you might tell other people about how you are experiencing things emotionally.

There are lots of reasons why people don't share their feelings. If you tend to bottle things up, see if any of the following strike a chord with you. You might remember some of these from earlier. (Notice how many *'shoulds'* occur here).

Some Reasons You Can't Say How You Feel

1. Conflict Phobia

You are afraid of angry feelings or conflicts with people, or you think if people are happy, they shouldn't disagree or argue.

2. Emotional Perfectionism

You set high standards for yourself and others when it comes to feelings; for example, feelings such as anger or jealousy are 'wrong'. You think you should always be in control of your emotions. You are afraid that if you show sadness or hurt, you will expose your vulnerability.

3. Fear of Disapproval and Rejection

You are so terrified by rejection and ending up alone that you would rather put up with something than risk someone getting angry with you. (The people-pleaser).

4. Passive-Aggressive Behaviour

You hold your hurt or angry feelings but instead of telling someone what you feel, you give them the silent treatment, to try to make them feel guilty.

5. Hopelessness

You are convinced that there's nothing you can do to improve the situation, so you give up trying. Of course, this could be a self-fulfilling prophecy – once you give up, the more likely it is that painful feelings will persist.

7. Getting out of control

You worry that once you start talking about why you are angry, hurt, jealous etc. things will spiral out of control, and you'll feel overwhelmed.

8. Mind Reading

You believe that others should know how you feel and what you need and if they don't, it shows they don't care about you.

9. Martyrdom

You are reluctant to admit that you are angry, hurt, or resentful because you do not want to give anyone the satisfaction of knowing that her or his behaviour has affected you.

10. Need to Solve Problems

When you have a conflict with an individual, instead of trying to understand each other, you view the situation as a problem that you need to fix, and you overlook the emotional dimension that underlies it.

All these ways of responding to/dealing with feelings could be challenged – see if you can work out ways to do this regarding your own behaviour.

Why is it a good thing to tell people about our feelings?

In general, it is now accepted that sharing your feelings, if this is done in a constructive way, without blame or criticism, can be very helpful because it enables you to experience a number of positive benefits:

- Being listened to helps you feel supported.
- It helps you to clarify and specify exactly what is happening for you at the time.
- Others can understand you better.
- It releases tension and anxiety and helps you to calm down, reducing activity in the amygdala.
- It may help you adjust your perspective and see things in a new way.
- You feel validated and heard, and perhaps understood better.
- You feel less lonely as a result.
- It stops you from ruminating, and maybe making the problem worse.
- Feelings which are worked through can be dealt with and their impact lessened; if they are simply 'managed' (i.e.: suppressed) they continue to affect you for a long time.
- It enables you to be honest and authentic in your relationships (no game-playing, manipulation or pretending).
- It clarifies any differences between you and someone else, in order to negotiate or resolve problems in a win-win way.
- It helps you and others to know what you want or need.
- It allows you to express yourself cleanly and directly without negatively affecting someone else.
- The feeling of being understood greatly enhances your sense of wellbeing.
- Your capacity to accept your own feelings also enhances your ability to empathise with other people and so improves relationships and deepens intimacy.
- If you acknowledge your vulnerability, others can get closer to you and care for you.

For a moment, let's go back to our brains: we now know that a lot of emotional processing takes place within the **prefrontal cortex**. The left side of the prefrontal cortex is concerned with verbal processes so can help us describe what happens in words (interestingly, it also tends to register more positive emotions). The right prefrontal cortex is more connected to the limbic system and helps us to understand the **meaning** of our emotions through metaphors and images; it processes visual information and non-verbal communication, as well as linking closely to the body's arousal system. In people who are emotionally literate, there are good connections between the left and right parts of their prefrontal cortex. When less emotionally aware people feel threatened by their feelings, they retreat into a 'left brain' as a form of defence. They may talk a lot but not really get into the full emotional experience. (Have you ever heard someone who has just experienced the loss of someone very dear saying something like, *'Oh well, I suppose it was going to happen sometime'*?)

The results of not accepting and expressing feelings fully include a lessened ability to work through feelings; people will talk about them in a somewhat superficial, linguistic way which can be rather arid and empty. Those feelings often continue to lurk below the surface.

How to share your feelings

You will get better at sharing your feelings the more you practise. It's important to recognise that this about **taking responsibility** for your feelings – owning them – and not blaming someone else for the way you feel. Even when you have problems with difficult feelings in relationships, remember that other people didn't *cause* these. (Just to underline this: if certain behaviour caused certain reactions, these would always be the same for everyone, but they're not! One person might hear a critical remark in a helpful way: e.g.: it gives them an opportunity to improve, while someone else might take it personally and be very upset. Yet others might become really angry. The different responses lie with the person receiving the remark, not the one sending it).

Ways to access and express feelings fully include:

If you are alone:

- Being **aware** of exactly which emotions you are experiencing, by building up a vocabulary of feelings words (see the emotions wheel on page 56) and naming them to yourself.
- Allowing yourself to **experience the full intensity** of the feeling, even if you temporarily get upset; it is known that crying releases oxytocin and other endorphins. These are feel-good chemicals which ease both physical and emotional pain, eventually leading to a sense of calm and wellbeing.
- Noticing the **physical effects** of these emotions and the intensity of your feelings by scaling them between 1 and 10, to help you recognise how serious or important they are. Note how they peak and fall.
- Allowing **silence** in order to get in touch with your inner experience; this might take you to an almost meditative state.
- Using **imagery and art** to describe feelings fully and get at deeper meanings that don't just rely on language to describe them.
- Acknowledging and **accepting** your feelings, speaking them out loud or writing them down if it helps.

If you are sharing with another person:

- **Choosing your moments**: it's best to save important disclosures for a time when you are calm, and the person you want to talk to is available and ready to listen. Flying off the handle rarely helps. (If you have to postpone the conversation because of your circumstances, you may temporarily **contain or regulate** your feelings – see below.)
- Choosing **someone who you trust** to be able to show empathy towards you and enable you to focus on yourself.
- Beginning with **'I'** – *'I feel…'* *'I would like…'* *'I am…'* – owning your feelings.
- **Avoiding distracting** from the emotion by rationalising, interpreting, or analysing in an intellectual way.
- Using tones of voice, eye contact, facial expressions etc. which are **adult**, (no childish whining, no 'parent-y' crossness!).
- **Not blaming** or criticising anyone else.

- Remember to share **positive emotions** as well as negative! By doing so, you will encourage more behaviour of the kind that provoked this positive reaction and good feeling.
- If you find your feelings overwhelming, or there is no-one in your life who you trust to share them with, consider seeking **therapy.**

It is probably still true to say that men generally tend to talk about or express their emotions less frequently than women. There is some research (see e.g., the book by John Gray – bibliography) which shows that men's and women's brains are made differently, and that levels of hormones also vary between men and women. (This may partly account for differences in the way they each handle emotions. Many men tend to withhold their feelings and it perhaps is not surprising that suicide rates tend to be high among young men. I can remember when I worked as a counsellor, seeing three different mums whose sons had taken their own lives; from each I heard repeatedly phrases such as, *'But why? I had no idea there was anything wrong!')*

An example

Remember Chris? Let's go back to an extract from our conversation and change it slightly to see if the therapist can help him to become aware of, and express, some emotions, instead of focusing on challenging his thoughts.

> **C:** "I'm scared nobody will like me.
> I've always hated meeting new people."

T: "It sounds as if this kind of feeling has been around a long time.
Can you explain a bit more about feeling scared?
What is the fear about?"

> **C:** "It reminds me of being a child.
> When I first went to secondary school,
> I remember feeling overwhelmed by
> all the things and people I didn't know.
> They all seemed ok but I was different."

T: "'Overwhelmed.'
That's a pretty strong word."

C: "Well, yes, but…nothing seemed safe.
I didn't know anyone; I didn't know how
to find my way around.
I felt like an outsider, excluded."

T: "That sounds very painful."

C: "Yeah. I felt lonely and helpless.
And that's the kind of feeling I get
when I start anything new – like this job."

Can you see how the therapist is trying to help Chris name the emotions he has and express them clearly? She's also interested in being as specific as possible about the intensity of the feeling - exploring what 'overwhelmed' means for Chris.

Later, Chris worries about other people's reactions to him. In working with his emotions, the therapist might help him focus more deeply on his experience, avoiding getting led into possible explanations for what might happen, other people's behaviour, or ways of dealing with unhelpful thinking.

C: "This confirms that people don't like me.
It doesn't matter how hard I've worked to get here,
they'll spot that I'm an impostor,
someone who doesn't belong."

T: "You would feel like an impostor
– someone who didn't deserve to be there.
What does that mean for you?"

C: "That I'm not good enough – a fraud who's useless and unlovable. They'll see through me and reject me."

T: "Unlovable.
Perhaps we need to just stay with this for a moment.
It feels really tender and sensitive."

While this is painful for Chris, once he allows his feelings to surface, and shares them, he finds that far from rejecting him, the therapist validates his experience and shows caring and understanding. The relationship enables him to feel accepted as he is.

EMOTIONAL REGULATION

You'll remember that we talked earlier about learning to tolerate the things we can't change. Acceptance means being willing to accept a situation as it is, rather than how we want it to be. That doesn't mean denying our feelings about events or situations, but it can require us to recognise that now might not be a good time to express them. If, for good reasons, we defer dealing with our feelings, we need to know how to contain them temporarily until the time comes to express them fully. To be able to cope with sudden powerful emotional reactions, it can help to learn certain skills that help us to regulate our emotions. (But remember to come back to them at some point so they don't accumulate in a toxic way.)

One example of a feeling we find hard to deal with is anger. Anger is a natural, normal human response when things don't go the way we'd like them to. Even a new-born baby can tell you this! It causes trouble when it is expressed in an unhelpful way. Angry behaviour appears to have a payoff for the angry person in that it gives them attention and a sense of control. However, this doesn't improve relationships! When people get angry, the emotion can affect them very powerfully and they may tend to:

- Judge, blame or criticise
- Call someone names or put them down
- Interrupt and refuse to listen

- Shout, gesticulate and threaten – even getting violent

- none of which helps the situation! However, suppressed anger can be extremely damaging to your wellbeing because of the amount of stress it generates. So, to help you to manage your anger and that of other people, or any strong feelings which can't be addressed immediately, consider the following ideas as a temporary measure:

1. **Distraction:** find something to do that will keep you busy and stop you ruminating on the problem. Preferably, let this be a fun activity rather than an onerous chore.

2. **Do good:** it is a truism that if you stop thinking about yourself and do something for someone else, you'll feel better; go out into the world and contribute something worthwhile.

3. **See the bigger picture**: recognise that this is one event within the continuum of your life. In the past, you have probably felt worse at some time; in the future, this will have passed, and you will have almost forgotten it.

4. Some emotions can be countered simply by **evoking the opposite one**: do something that makes you laugh; find something calming to soothe you down.

5. **Limit your worry time**: if you must think about something, set aside a specific time to do this and then put it away for the rest of the day. Worry never changed anything!

6. **Accept the problem**; whatever your wishes might be, some things just don't work out the way you would like them to. This doesn't mean you have to like it but perhaps you can decide not to let it spoil your 'now' time. Life is full of ups and downs and no matter what you do, you won't be happy all the time!

7. Behave in ways that make you **feel good about yourself**. If you can respond with calm dignity instead of flying off the handle, if you can learn to take compassionate care of yourself when you're unhappy, or show kindness to others even when their behaviour seems inappropriate, you will at least feel pleased to be the kind of person you are.

8. Always **check facts** if an incident provokes you; if you are responsible for anything which seems on reflection to have been unhelpful, own it and apologise if necessary.

9. **Learn resilience**: find ways to bounce back from setbacks: talk to yourself about anything you might learn from a disappointing situation; remind yourself of the qualities you have that have helped you to recover and teach yourself new skills that might help you do better next time.

10. De-stress by **doing something physical** – even if it's just walking outside for a few minutes.

11. **Slow down**! You'd be surprised just how much talking in a lower, slower voice and breathing slowly will calm you physically.

12. If someone else is involved, try to put yourself in their situation and see it from their **point of view**. What makes them behave that way?

13. Remember what gives your **life meaning**; at the end of the day, what are the most important things to you?

THE ROLE OF THERAPY

Sometimes, perhaps because the problems in your relationships have become very complex, or because you feel you have already taken up a lot of someone's time but still feel a need to be listened to (as can happen following a loss, for example), you may benefit from talking to someone independent and neutral. Some of the advantages of talking therapy over self-help include:

- The time is set aside specifically for you, and it's not self-indulgent or wrong to spend the entire time looking at your issues.

- The therapist is not involved in your life or biased in any way; (s)he will offer a non-judgemental approach to what you talk about and will help you to feel validated.

- Confidentiality (apart from in a few exceptional cases) is guaranteed so you know (s)he won't talk about you to anyone else (apart from his/her professional supervisor).

- If you find a therapist you feel comfortable with, (s)he will offer a warm, caring relationship in which you will feel valued and supported.

- You can move at your own pace, go over things as much as you like and stay silent when that feels right.
- You can express even strong or scary feelings that you might not want to share with anyone else.

There are many different therapists out there, and they work in a myriad of different ways. In general, you will tend to find that some might call themselves 'Person-Centred': they work very much with feelings, as in the last extract from Chris's therapy, and focus on your unique experiences; CBT therapists emphasise the value of working with unhelpful thinking and behaviours (Chris's first extract); psychodynamic therapists are interested in the relevance of your past experiences to the way you are living your life now. For many therapists, especially as they develop more knowledge and experience, training in all these areas can become integrated in such a way that they can draw on a range of skills to try and match their interventions to their clients' needs as closely as possible. If you are seeking a therapist, it's a good idea to ask about their theoretical orientation.

You might also consider the personal qualities that you might look for in a therapist. This is very much about feeling comfortable with them, in order feel safe and trusting. Probably the most valuable quality is empathy. Is this someone who seems as if they might really try to understand you, and to see the world from your perspective? Do they seem as if they would grasp the meanings of what you say and maybe even find underlying meaning to things which you're hardly aware of? Does (s)he seem able to 'hold' whatever you bring, no matter how intense the emotion attached to it? I would always suggest you ask for an introductory session before you commit to regular therapy.

Section 14

PAUSE FOR THOUGHT: THE BIGGER PICTURE

We have spent most of the discussion so far talking about you as an individual and this largely follows the philosophy of the self-esteem movement, which tends to encourage focus on the individual. This is where I'm going to throw in a personal view which challenges the emphasis on self-esteem and which you might take exception to – but hear me out, and then make up your own mind.

In recent years, a great deal has been said, written and researched about 'self-esteem' and the assumption has grown up that it can only be good to develop a strong sense of self-esteem in order to strengthen your mental wellbeing. Indeed, it would seem that this is what this book is about.

However, I'd like to stress that I am not encouraging an 'I, myself and me' approach to life! For sure, we all need to feel that there is meaning to our lives, that we matter and receive validation. Ideally, as we have seen, this is provided first within the relationship with our primary caregivers. People for whom this was not available often experience mental health difficulties later and may require help to develop their potential for happiness and good relationships. Therapy and self-help tend to be directed towards this. However, all this focus on the *self* can, paradoxically, lead to various unhelpful outcomes.

For instance:

- Someone might become unhealthily self-absorbed, talking endlessly about their feelings and their problems, and become less aware of others and the outside world.
- Constantly re-visiting their problems and 'telling their story' doesn't necessarily enable them to improve difficult situations but may even keep them where they are!
- They might 'wallow' in their perceived victimhood as if this somehow defines them, and even see the expression of noisy or highly visible displays of emotion as imbued with some kind of virtue; emoting of itself does not bring about change (except maybe bringing a very temporary relief!)
- They might look for a magic bullet to solve their problems instead of developing their own resources and taking responsibility for helping themselves.
- They may become socially disconnected, missing out on shared experiences and shared benefits, and unable to empathise with others.
- Many people may develop a false sense of their significance in the world (perhaps fostered by their behaviour on social media).
- For some, their own views and opinions are given such significance that they think the rest of the world should change to get in line with these.
- Often, people become overly concerned with appearance and self-image; they may feel negatively judged in terms of certain aspects of their appearance; this can actually lead to further psychological distress.
- Some people may not appreciate and foster the good things they have.
- In seeking what they think they are entitled to, some people become less tolerant of anything which interferes with their gratification, and lose sight of the fact that, in general, you need to put something *in* before you can take something *out*.
- Some may not recognise the adverse effects of their behaviour on other people.

- The pursuit of 'happiness' becomes something they feel entitled to even if this results in: 1 - risky behaviour (e.g.: when driving, taking drugs). 2 - anti-social attitudes - disrespecting others to get what they want. 3 - not being satisfied with anything ordinary or mundane.

- Seeking a constant dopamine hit can be the way addiction starts.

TAKING A WIDER-WORLD PERSPECTIVE

I'm not saying here that fostering self-esteem is a bad thing, so much as that our self-esteem is linked to a very large extent of our connections with other people. We are all part of a community and society at large; our individual wellbeing depends, at least in part, on how healthy that society is. Understanding about sharing, give-and-take, tolerance and so on is just as important as looking after ourselves. Please indulge me while I expand further on this.

What the self-esteem movement tends to neglect is the **social side** of human existence. Everything we do connects to the world and other people in some way. While you may look out and see other people, remember that they look back in and see you! I'm going to offer a few suggestions now about how your mental and emotional wellbeing might be helped by taking a more outward-looking view and moving away from introspection:

1. Think about all those 'bubbles' in the covid crisis; remember how much people said they missed each other; remember how wonderful things happened, where neighbourhoods worked together to support their more vulnerable members; how people gave so much at their places of work to enable us all to rise to the challenge of the pandemic; how attitudes of gratitude and praise were fostered...

My contention is that this crisis required people to think outside themselves as individuals and look at the bigger picture. Suddenly their relationships with other people became highlighted and the endeavours they undertook were about the community and the common good. Those who participated in doing good (care-workers, nurses, food bank volunteers and so on) realised their own contribution to the world was important and this was acknowledged within society. They *did* something and the rewards for themselves in terms of recognition and feeling valued arose because they helped everyone else!

2. In the area where I live, there are very many small schools. Some of the tiniest village schools are actually the most successful, not just in OFSTED terms, but because of the ways that the people within them behave together. You go in and you can pick up at once on the happy atmosphere and the positive attitudes of the pupils. Why is this? Many Heads I've spoken to refer to the 'family atmosphere' and talk about everyone knowing each other. What is very striking is that each person is able to see the impact of their own behaviour. Often this is overtly discussed in a variety of ways – not just with stickers and charts, but in meaningful conversations and a deliberate focus on consequences, both good and bad, and learning about their part in this microcosm of society. There is a pride in belonging and in maintaining the group identity.

Feeling that the members of organisations are interdependent is good for society and the kinds of qualities this fosters encourage development within individuals too. These qualities include: being able to delay gratification and work towards goals through extended effort; a valuing of curiosity, and a sense of adventure; self-control, self-reliance and self-discipline. Shared values, common goals and personal responsibility link together to enable a stable society. The more you cut yourself off from community, the more isolated you are likely to become.

3. You may remember Caroline Flack, who hosted 'Love Island' and won 'Strictly.' She tragically hanged herself in 2020, and yet on the surface she had everything young people seem to aspire to – beauty, success, money. You can google many examples of famous people ('celebrities') being unable to cope with the very things they thought they wanted.

There is a tendency today to promote the idea that we each can be 'special', 'amazing', 'the best' and so on, perhaps fostered by programmes like talent shows and the general celebrity culture. Our young people seem to have stronger aspirations to be the next highly paid star than to be someone who plays a valuable part in society. Ironically, many celebrities reveal in some way that they have mental health problems. Perhaps what is at fault here is the notion that happiness is about being beautiful, rich, or famous. Or maybe people expect to be 'happy' in ways that are simply not realistic. What can be true is that if you constantly focus on your own gratification, you may actually become disconnected from other people and all that that implies.

My dad always encouraged me to work hard at school and wanted me to attend a 'good' university. My grades were very important, but then came the fatal day when the A level results arrived. Horror of horrors! I had failed one so didn't meet the entry criteria for university. I can still remember the maelstrom of feelings I experienced following this 'failure' and it took a long, long time to recover from it. Looking back on this now, I can see so much that contributed to my discomfort: I had always been labelled 'bright' and was therefore expected to do 'better' than other people; I was anxious to please my parents in order to feel loved by them; my efforts to be successful had become the measure of my self-worth; no-one suggested that I might enjoy the work for its own sake, or to develop my curiosity and love of learning. Children who are academically successful are often treated as if they're special. It is similar for sportspeople (who is 'man of the match?') or writers and artists (think bestsellers lists/awards/exhibiting in prestigious galleries).

Sometimes, when people are disappointed in some way you may hear them crying that they should have been given greater support (blaming)/shouldn't be expected to do the kinds of things others have to do (work hard for something)/have reasons to be excused responsibility (felt tired, no time, unwell…). Conversely, there are people who will regale you with a list of their 'rights', and what 'should' have been done for them. Sometimes, focusing on self too much can lead to someone feeling that they must have special allowances made for them. They have developed a sense of **entitlement** because the notion that they are less able/shouldn't need to help themselves, has been fostered.

Other people may explain away some crime or misdemeanour by saying they have **difficulties** which 'led to' the unacceptable behaviour, as if they are powerless to make choices. Even at a minor level, some may treat other people badly, by being late, by not responding to communications, by being

JENNY OYSTON

abusive or disrespectful and generally letting others down. They might justify this by saying they've 'had a hard time' or they've been 'feeling low'. They have clear ideas about how they want others to treat them, but don't model this in the way they themselves behave.

Undoubtedly life hands out more curve balls to some people than to others. In a well-balanced society, we would all wish to support the most vulnerable and those with different needs. However, what seems to have got lost somewhere is that old maxim that you get out what you put in. Is it unreasonable to expect some contribution towards the common good to be made by everyone, whatever their circumstances? Is being the star better than being a member of the team? We do see some shining examples - people who have suffered appalling injuries doing wonderful work for charity, people who continue through voluntary work to give to the community long after their paid working life, and so on. My concern is that, if we start to suggest that having 'mental health problems' is a reason *not* to do something, we actually contribute to the problem rather than alleviate it, because the sufferer may become lethargic, dependent, unmotivated and devalued!

Finally, consider the effect of developing a '**non-judgemental attitude**' (as many therapists advocate): is it realistic to expect inappropriate behaviour not to be challenged? While enjoying someone's achievements can we not also suggest ways to get even better? When people act against society, is it enough to try to 'understand' this without trying to rectify it? (Note I talk about *behaviour* here: I'm not advocating judging *people*).

What sort of feedback is most helpful? Instead of using labels (such as those on page 17) wise teachers use their praise for the effort, commitment, persistence and so on that their pupils put in, not simply for apparently innate gifts or talents; more importantly, they see their students' learning as an enjoyable and worthwhile process and use 'mistakes' as learning and development opportunities. So as a therapist, I want to help my clients to identify the strengths and qualities they can use to enable their growth; I encourage commitment to the process; I want them to be able to celebrate new discoveries about themselves and to challenge themselves to even

132

greater development through self-agency! I will feel I've done a good job if my clients develop:

- **Compassion** for themselves and others.
- **Acceptance** of things they can't change.
- **Responsibility** for their own self-development.
- **Efficacy:** ability to use their skills to make desirable changes and choices.

Section 15

WHAT HAVE YOU LEARNT ABOUT YOURSELF SO FAR?

By this point, I hope you have a clearer idea of which aspects of your life you might want to change or develop. It's worth pausing before we move on to part three, to see if you have been able to identify what your priorities are now, in the light of all we've been looking at. I invite you to complete the following questionnaire to clarify your thinking in preparation for exploring ways of actually carrying out what you want to do in order to improve your wellbeing.

QUESTIONNAIRE: WHERE AM I NOW? An inventory of what you know about yourself and what you'd like to change.

To complete this, look at the topics in columns 1 and 2 and tick the boxes in column 3 if the aspect named is something you'd like to change. (Don't choose too many!) Finally, when you have been right through the questions, identify priorities: in column 4 put 1 for short-term/high priority, 2 for medium term/medium priority, 3 for long-term/less urgent. It is best if you have a few short-term priorities, fewer medium- and long-term ones. You can come back to this as often as you want, and don't be afraid to add your own ideas to either of the first two columns.

AREA OF WELLBEING	FEATURES/ASPECTS OF THIS AREA	WOULD LIKE TO CHANGE (TICK)	PRIORITY 1, 2 OR 3
Aspects of self	Roles I play.		
	My strengths and qualities.		

	Relationships I currently have.		
Values	Living according to values.		
	My prejudices.		
	Labels I use.		
Beliefs	Challenging messages from the past.		
	Exploring underlying beliefs.		
	Understanding my culture and influences from the past.		
Aspects of Experience	Knowing how behaviour, thoughts, physical factors and emotions interact.		
Thinking styles	Recognising the role of unhelpful thinking in my behaviour.		
Behaviour styles	Understanding my behaviour style as assertive/passive/ aggressive.		
Emotions	Understanding my emotions:		
	Family and environmental influences.		
	Links to behaviour.		

	Triggers.		
	Emotional awareness.		
Happiness	Maintaining a good work/life balance.		
	Resources.		
	Finding meaning.		
	Exploring areas which contribute to my happiness.		
Accepting	Coming to terms with things I must accept and making the choice to change what I can.		
Physical Condition	Developing my physical health:		
	Diet, sleep, exercise, relaxation.		
Challenging thoughts and beliefs	Eliminating should/ought/must.		
	Unhelpful thinking to be noted and challenged.		
Helpful behaviour patterns	Taking responsibility for my behaviour.		
	Practising assertive behaviour to deal with conflict, saying no, asking for what I want, handling criticism.		

	Introducing relaxation techniques.		
	Exploring mindfulness.		
	Demonstrating affection.		
	Planning new achievements – work and leisure.		
	Building new relationships.		
Emotional expression and regulation	Dealing with strong feelings in a healthy way.		
	Learning to share and express feelings.		
	Learning emotional regulation techniques when needed.		
Bigger picture	Contribution to society What might I be able to give?		

Section 16

WHERE DO YOU GO FROM HERE?

Let's re-cap on what we've discussed so far:

In part one, I invited you to explore the person you are now. We looked at the roles you play, the values you hold and your beliefs. We briefly explored how you came to be the person you are today. Then we went into greater detail about the way you think and behave. We spent some time attempting to understand the origins and effects of your emotions and then I asked you to think about happiness and what it means to you. I hope that from all this exploration, you were able to find areas of your life that you wanted to change or develop.

In part two, I started from the premise that there are some things we may not be able to change, and the idea that acceptance is a helpful way to respond to these. We then spent some time thinking about possible ways of improving various aspects of your life, from physical wellbeing, to thoughts and beliefs, to behaviour, especially in difficult situations. Lastly, we looked again at emotions, from the perspective of being able to handle strong feelings in a helpful way.

Finally, I made a plea for looking at the bigger picture – focusing on a wider society beyond yourself and looking externally to the outside world, rather than focusing solely on yourself and your internal experiences. I suggested that you might turn your attention outwards, and include looking at the part you play in the community and the world at large.

Following all this discussion, you might like to take the opportunity to re-evaluate some of the answers you put to the questions and exercises in part one. So before we move on to the section about how to get where you want to, I invite you to re-visit your values, beliefs, thinking patterns and so on and see whether you still espouse those you identified in the early part of the book. What fundamental lessons have come out of your self-discovery? Has your philosophy of life changed at all? Do you have a clearer idea of the fundamental principles that underlie your behaviour? If you were to write a character study of the person you'd like to be, what would it be like? In other words, ask yourself again:

WHO AM I?

WHO DO I WANT TO BE?

HOW DO I GET THERE?

ARE YOU READY TO DO THIS?

I hope by now that you have got an idea of some of the things you'd like to do differently. There's a lot you can do to make your life more enjoyable and fulfilling, but let's not pretend there's a quick fix, or that it's easy. If you really want to overhaul your mental wellbeing, you need to:

1. Discard any sense of entitlement: while in theory, everyone has the right to 'be the best they can be' as the jargon has it, be assured: you won't get it by doing nothing.
2. Accept that you're ordinary: you're no more special than anyone else; if people tell you that you can be 'amazing' or 'incredible,' listen with a healthy dose of scepticism: however good you are, even if you work hard on your development, you will not be 'better' than anyone else as a person.
3. Realise that you're the one who needs to do the work; even the most gifted, talented people will make nothing of their gifts if they don't cultivate them; this involves commitment, risk, and some unpredictability - even with the greatest effort, things won't always go as you'd like (though you can find support if you're prepared to look for it). Don't expect to see a change if you don't make one!
4. Forget the idea that mistakes = failure. Mistakes are where the learning happens! Don't ask, 'what went wrong?' Ask, 'what can I learn from that?'
5. You will need reserves of resilience and persistence to get you through the tough times as well as a capacity for gratitude when you are successful.
6. Grow the ability to discard any reliance on the judgement of others; while it's nice to receive positive feedback, you don't have to please anyone else; your own feelings about yourself and your behaviour are the best guide: aim for integrity.
7. Connect with others and take responsibility for them as well as yourself.
8. Once you start, this will become a lifelong journey - but you'll enjoy it! Don't stop every time you think you've achieved something - seek a new challenge.
9. **MAKE A COMMITMENT!**

The real pleasure will come from learning along the way – finding ways to develop your interests and abilities, extending your understanding of yourself, behaving in ways that are in tune with your moral and ethical values, improving relationships…the list goes on!

How Do I Get There?

~ PART THREE ~

Section 17

GOALS: DO THEY HELP US?

I have always had a problem with goals. I remember once on a training course, asking a very eminent psychologist why she set so much store by goals. She said to me, 'Well, if you don't have goals, how do you know where you're going?'

How do we choose the route we take, and what are the consequences of these choices? Imagine you are standing at that crossroads now; where do you want to go, and how might you get there?

The 'for and against' of goal setting:

In favour of goals	Why goals may not be helpful
Goals motivate you and give you something to aspire to.	They might come from somewhere outside of you: teachers, parents, employers etc.
Outcomes can be broken down into smaller steps so that you can see a clear pathway ahead.	You may get stuck chasing something which you no longer find fulfilling.
You can measure your success as each stage is achieved.	You may get preoccupied with the fail/succeed dichotomy and miss the real growth in learning.

You can share your aspirations with those around you and gain their support.	It becomes all about outcome/end product and you don't enjoy the 'journey.'
Your goals can provide a realistic picture of where you are now and where you might get to.	You may narrow your focus so much that you overlook other opportunities.
You can take charge of your own progress and monitor your success and achievements.	Depending on your learning style, fixed goals may not be flexible enough.
You can take an overview of the factors relevant to your success (try a SWOT analysis, looking at: strengths, weaknesses, opportunities, threats) and be prepared.	You could end up with unwelcome labels like 'good at' or 'not able' which overlooks your pleasure in an activity.
You can give yourself a clear time frame.	You may feel you have to be in competition with others or limit your activity because of restrictions others or other factors impose.

I find I lean towards the right-hand column. I feel I always want to follow the less-travelled route, and I love surprises. When I'm in a new place, I don't like being confined by fences, and want to explore those intriguing little paths that go off to the side. I don't go for beaches with brollies, but coves you have to scramble down to. What about you? Does having clear goals feel more comfortable to you or are you a wanderer?

For the goal-setters among you, there are all sorts of guides you can follow. I offer some suggestions on the next few pages. Whether you want to set goals, formally or not, you may like to have with you the list of priorities you had identified by the time you reached the end of part two.

THE PROCESS OF GOAL SETTING

If every journey begins with the first step, we must stop prevaricating and make a **plan**! Some people like to do this formally, others work in a freer, more flexible way. Whichever you prefer, I suggest that the important elements of a manageable plan include:

- **Identify changes** you would like to make (call these your 'goals'); be fairly free about this, just putting on paper whatever looks like fun /useful/challenging/stimulating etc. Remember to address all aspects of your wellbeing, including physical, social, emotional, and spiritual; don't just make it about *doing*.

- **Put them in order** – maybe in terms of *priorities* or according to the time they need; or, to motivate you, start with something small which you can achieve fairly easily and build up gradually to the big ones. All change involves a certain level of risk, but if some things appear too difficult, work out why and don't be afraid to put them on hold for the time being.

- **Research what you need:** e.g.: you might need to look around for some kind of support, or to see what training is available locally, or do some background reading and note-making.

- Often, changes we make affect other people; think through any 'sensitive' **conversations** you may need to have. This particularly applies to relationship situations, whether personal or at work. If you are going to need, say, more time to carry out your plans, you will need to think about who else this might affect.

When you have made your list of goals, review them, get feedback, and see if you want to make any adjustments. You might group your goals under the heading of long, medium, and short-term, and set dates for when you will achieve them. Other people make *SMART* goals. In a nutshell, these are:

- **Specific** – clear about what you want to accomplish.
- **Measurable** – having some way of knowing when you make progress.
- **Achievable** – thinking about other factors in your life, the goal is something you are likely to be able to do.

- **Relevant** – the goal needs to lead to your doing something that will make your life better.
- **Time** – bound: realistic in terms of when you might achieve it.

Some people build a regular review process into their plan. This can be helpful, because if things don't go as you hope, you can examine what brought about this unexpected result. This may be useful in preventing you from giving up. Don't spend too long on the planning – this may just be procrastination in disguise!

It is really helpful at this point to write your goals down. (It's like having a shopping list; with my non-goal driven approach, I might come home with a lovely new pudding; my husband would only seek out the things we wrote down.)

How your record your goals is up to you. If I were working with Chris to help him feel integrated and accepted in his new job, one of the goals we might identify could be recorded like the example on the next page.

EXAMPLE:

Long-term goal: feel accepted as a member of the team		
Short-term steps	**What I need to do**	**Helpful resources and strategies**
Find a 'friend' among colleagues	Start a conversation: Ask about his/her likes about the job. Enquire about family. Listen and respond to replies. Offer support/help with tasks/making coffee etc. Tell them a bit about me.	Practising with people I know. Reading about ways of making conversation - self-help books. Keeping a journal to record what works. Practising calming strategies.
Review: Look back after two weeks and see how this went: would I do anything differently? Record/acknowledge successes		
Use what I've learnt with two others in the team, then continue to branch out and explore other relationships.	Observe the dynamics of the team and the roles people play. Decide who looks interesting to me and resolve to get to know them better. Focus my interest on them - what they do at work and at home.	Reading about group processes and how people interact. Continuing to develop my self-awareness - what kinds of people appeal to me? Increasing my ability to listen well and to empathise. Attending a course on active listening.

Suggest doing something with someone I feel confident with.	Invite a colleague I find friendly to an event/outing etc.	Research about what's going on in the area and ensure you know times etc.
Review: Explore how this went, monitoring my own responses and emotional reactions: what felt good/ scary/ challenging etc? Has my ability to mix improved? (Scale from 1- 10)		
Repeat the steps above until I reach a 'comfort level.'	Accept what feels realistic in this situation – not everyone will like me. Learn to live with the reality that I won't be close to everyone.	Using self-compassion: focus on what is working. Reading about human behaviour and how people make relationships.
Continue to review formally and informally so that my understanding is always growing. Observe people around me and get a sense of how they make relationships; use this as a model.		

You can see that this provides lots of material for further work.

LIFE PLAN

Before we finish looking at goals, it may help you to think about the bigger picture, by writing an overall **life plan**: Think about how your life was, is, and could be, in relation to different aspects. Take each area and consider it in different periods in time, like this:

Aspect of Life	5 Years Ago	Now	5 Years from Now
Where you live			
Who you live with			
Social Life			
Interests and Hobbies			
Your Jobs and Ambitions			
Financial Security			
Health			
Emotional Health			
Physical Fitness			
Self-Acceptance			
Community Roles			

Incidentally, I'm not sure about whether this is a good thing, but some people create a list of 50 things to do before they die, or a bucket list. Would you want to do this?

Section 18

MONITORING YOUR PROGRESS: SELF-REFLECTION

Even if we didn't work on a life-plan together in a such a formal, structured way, one thing I would always encourage is the keeping of a **journal**. I personally prefer this method of self-development to having a rigid plan, because it's flexible and centred on real day-to-day experience. Journaling is helpful in so many ways:

- It enables you to stand back and reflect on what has happened.
- You can choose your focus – if something particularly affects you on a given day, you can explore it soon after the event.
- You will be able to better identify the parts you are responsible for, and what is down to circumstances or other people.
- You can accept your feelings and reactions without judgement.
- It can be cathartic to 'discharge' any strong emotions by writing them down.
- You can identify and appreciate progress and positive change.
- As you progress, you will be able to see development, however gradual, and clarify what you want next.

Clients often bring their journals to counselling so that they can also receive another person's reflections on events. It's also worth saying, that as people get to know and understand themselves better, they learn so much that they come to realise that any goals they set had set out at the start either no longer apply, or no longer matter! (I used to think it was so important always to get A*s that I would spend hours and hours 'perfecting' assignments. On 2 occasions when working towards qualifications, I really thought I was in line for distinctions, but missed each by a single mark. This was disappointing at first but I found that nobody ever asked afterwards what scores or grades I got and that I managed to get the jobs I wanted at the time even without distinctions, because what people interviewing were far more interested in was the candidate's personal qualities. I could have been out in the garden for a lot more time instead of sweating over a keyboard!)

So, how does the process of writing and learning from a journal help?

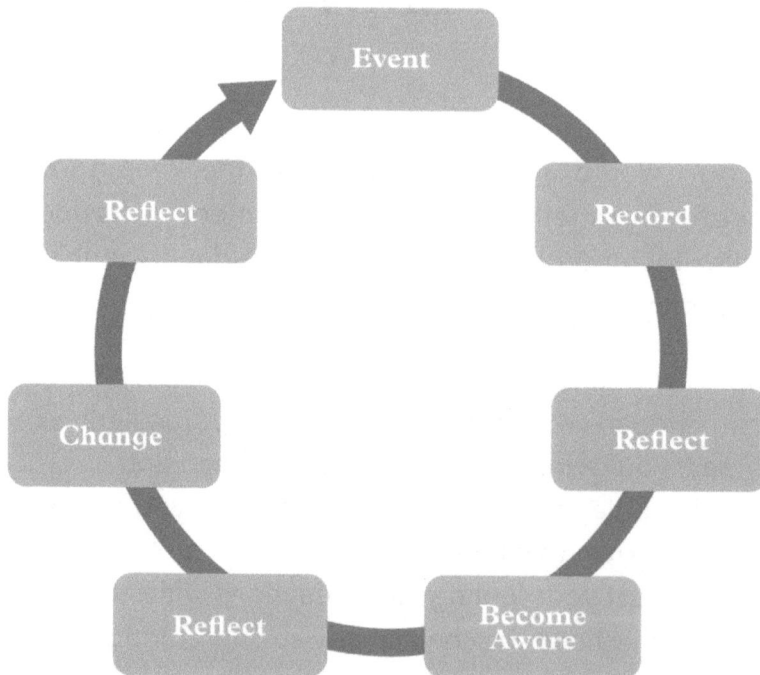

Looking at this diagram, you can see how the emphasis is on reflecting, learning about and understanding what happens when you experience events in your life. The purpose is to enable you to focus on your responses in order to see where and how you would like to make changes. Ideally, this self-reflection becomes a regular habit, so let's see how it might work in practice.

I suggest to Chris that when he starts his new job, he could keep a record or log of his experiences for us to look at. Throughout his day, it will help if he can tune in to his emotional and physical reactions to pick up any signs that he is especially affected by particular events which he can then reflect on later. This means 'stepping back' from them, and simply noticing what is going on for him at the time. Later, he can write about them in more detail. When completing the journal, it sometimes helps to have a particular focus for his attention, so that he doesn't find the task too overwhelming. I suggest that the focus could be on:

- What happened – describe this factually.
- Thinking and reflecting on why he's selected this event.
- Enhancing his self-awareness by exploring his emotions, his thoughts, his physical sensations and his behaviour when this happened.
- Reflecting on the above and exploring what he has learnt about himself from this.
- Asking whether he would like to make any changes in how he deals with such situations and deciding on some definite strategies to help him with similar situations in future.
- Reflecting on the whole situation again, then preparing to go back out into the world and being ready to face further events.

Here is an extract from the possible conversation we might have about a particular day's journal entry:

T: "Chris, have you written about an event that happened at work that you'd like to talk about?"

C: "Yes. I went into the admin office to ask someone to write a letter to a client for me."

T: "What made you choose this situation to look at?"

C: "Well, before I went in, I realised I was feeling really nervous. I don't know anyone in there yet, and they all looked really busy. I didn't want to be a nuisance."

T: "When you were writing your journal, did you record your responses in detail? What about physical sensations?"

C: "Yeah. I could feel a kind of tightness in my stomach, and I sort of clenched my jaw. It was like I was preparing for a struggle."

T: "And the emotions?"

C: "I was scared...it was like going to the headteacher's office when I was little."

T: "Can you say what you were scared of?"

C: "Well, basically, their reactions – they might ignore me, they might get irritated, they might put me down in some way."

T: "Did you manage to recall and record any of the thoughts you had at the time?"

C: "I've put down:
'They'll reject me and treat me disrespectfully.'
'I'm hopeless at asking for things like this.'
'I wish I was someone who people like seeing.'"

T: "So, what did you actually do?"

C: "I knocked on the door, but no-one answered so I just went in. One lady looked up at me, so I went towards her. I apologised for interrupting her. I felt as if everyone was looking at me so I quickly asked her to do the letter and then I left as quickly as I could."

T: "You have recorded all this in great detail. Well done. Now that we're looking back at it, have you learnt anything about yourself and how you handled the situation and why?"

At this point, Therapist and Chris spend a lot of time going over the various aspects of how Chris experienced and processed the entire episode, and you may imagine the thought challenging that goes on. Chris could later record this in his journal, so he can look back on it. They then might go on to consider strategies that could help Chris in future, when he is faced with new challenges. Again, it is helpful to record these - and not to over-burden him so that failure is more likely. On this occasion, they may focus together on:

- Ways to calm himself physically – taking a pause, using relaxed breathing, using mindfulness to keep him in the present.
- Trying to balance his thoughts by identifying positives (in the above situation, the admin lady did help him; he did achieve what he set out to achieve and he overcame his anxiety).
- Looking at the reality of the situation (he's not in school now; nobody has actually been hostile to him).
- Identifying his feelings and then regulating them by scaling and by talking to himself in a compassionate way (*It's OK to be nervous but I have the resources to overcome my nerves*).
- Behaving as if he were confident e.g.: by using posture, body language and facial expressions like confident people do: acting *as if* he is confident can feel like he actually *is*!
- Speaking assertively when asking for what he wants.

Chris could then continue to monitor how he deals with more new situations and gradually he will find that he gets better at making requests. It is important that he records his successes and achievements as he goes along.

One last thing – if you are not someone who enjoys writing, you can use **other media** to help you with self-reflection. Various forms of art could be helpful, including painting, collage, sculpture and photography. Colours and textures can be particularly evocative, and you could also work in metaphors and symbols of various kinds. For instance, a flowing river, a bridge, a violent storm can all relate to our feelings. Some people like to take a symbol from nature, such as a butterfly, to represent change. You could draw yourself in different situations – going on a journey with different adventures and challenges, creating an imaginary place to live, with comforting and protective things around you, and so on.

Nowadays, using digital media can be interesting, and you may develop new skills by working with images. How about making a series of PowerPoint slides about your life? Or taking a photo of yourself and manipulating it in different ways? Print photographic images of beautiful things to have around you.

Section 19

EMBARKING ON THE PROCESS OF CHANGE

I hope that by this stage you have identified a number of changes you might be able to put into place in your life and are starting to work out how you might do this. Of course, now the challenge to begin this process really starts! No-one else can do this for you, although many people will support you if you share with them what you're doing.

As I hinted above, one of the barriers to this might be the dreaded **procrastination**! I see a lot of clients who have ideas about what they'd like to do, but they don't seem able to get started. I remind them that they can only be sure of the here-and-now: the past can't be re-written, and the future is unknown. So, it has to be now!

In his book 'Being Happy', Andrew Matthews offers this short story which to me seems really poignant; it was written by an 85-year-old man who found out that he was dying:

If I had my life to live over again, I'd try to make more mistakes next time. I wouldn't be so perfect. I would relax more. I'd limber up.
I'd be sillier than I've been on this trip. In fact, I know very few things that I would take so seriously. I'd be crazier. I'd be less hygienic.

I'd take more chances, I'd take more trips, I'd climb more mountains, I'd swim more rivers, I'd go more places I've never been to. I'd eat more ice-cream and fewer beans. I'd have more actual troubles and fewer imaginary ones!

You see, I was one of those people who lived prophylactically and sensibly and sanely hour after hour and day after day. Oh, I've had my moments, and if I had to do it over again, I'd have more of those moments – moment by moment by moment.

I've been one of those people who never went anywhere without a thermometer, a hot water bottle, a gargle, a raincoat and a parachute. If I had it to do all over again, I'd travel lighter next time.

If I had it to do all over again, I'd start barefoot earlier in the spring and stay way later in the fall. I'd ride more merry-go-rounds, I'd watch more sunrises, and I'd play with more children, if I had my life over again.

But you see, I don't.

STAND UP TO PROCRASTINATION!

These ideas, some of which go back to things we looked at earlier in the book, may help:

- One of the reasons we procrastinate is that the **balance** of our lives is wrong. We don't have enough rewards or good experiences to make up for the chores and tedious jobs which consume our energy. How much time do you spend away from work and responsibility, engaged with people and activities you enjoy? It is useful to create a pie chart (See Page 61), to look at how you use your time, over any 24-hour period. Draw it out with sections showing how much of your day is taken up with different activities.

If necessary, change it so you have a better mix. Look at your plans for each day, checking that there is a healthy balance; if there are lots of mundane things to do or if you have long working hours, **structure your time**: plan to punctuate activities with 'wellbeing' breaks – go out in the fresh air, have a cup of tea, listen to an uplifting song.

- Another reason could be that the task ahead and the effort required just seem so enormous. It's a cliché to say that *the longest journey begins with the first step*, but it's true! So go back to your goals, if necessary, and break them down into smaller steps. Then – **do something**, however small, to get you started.

- Revisit what you learnt about unhelpful 'rules' and beliefs and tell yourself that: *whether you think you will succeed or not, you're right!* **Challenge unhelpful thinking**, especially around 'failing' and your understanding of what 'failure' is: remember that *if you learn something, even if it's not what you expected, you will have gained something positive.* Stop being a perfectionist and recognise that 'good enough' is all you need!

- The **labels** you give yourself are holding you back: *if you say you're lazy, incapable, incompetent, then that's how you'll be:* take those labels off!

CHOOSE TO BE POSITIVE!

Your attitude can make a tremendous difference to how you see the world and will influence your expectations about what you may be able to change. If you can develop a positive outlook (which is still realistic!) you will find life gets easier and more enjoyable. You can become more positive by:

- Nurturing a positive and compassionate attitude towards yourself.
- Cultivating an attitude of gratitude - be thankful for the good things in your day.
- Focusing on your strengths and qualities.
- Every evening, reminding yourself of at least 3 positives from that day.
- Reflecting thoughtfully on things that happen and listing what went well and what you enjoyed; examine how you played a part in making this happen.
- Rewarding your successes and sharing them with someone who cares.
- Cultivating qualities of perseverance, resilience, determination, persistence.
- Being kind to others and getting involved with the world.

When it comes to behaviour, there is a positive or a negative way of doing almost anything. Fill in the missing boxes in this list to remind you what you can do instead of behaving unhelpfully:

Positive behaviour	Negative behaviour
Eating a healthy diet	Eating junk/ 'comfort' eating
Exercising every day	Taking transport/sitting around
Doing something relaxing	Being a workaholic
	Feeling hurt because of listening to others' opinions
	Keeping your anger inside
	Feeling bored and fed up
	Getting into debt
	Saying bad things to yourself
	Thinking it's weak to cry
	Comparing yourself badly to other people
	Keeping your opinions to yourself so others don't consider you
	Expecting yourself and everyone else to behave perfectly all the time
	Expecting yourself to fail, so never really preparing for challenges

	Withdrawing love and affection as a way of trying to get noticed
	Refusing to communicate
	Punishing people for being 'wrong'
	Showing prejudice and making judgements
	Complaining, moaning, running things and people down
	Making people feel small
	Taking life too seriously
	Being lazy
	Expecting things from society without putting anything back

Whatever choices you make, these are up to you! If you see something in the right-hand column that you do regularly, commit to doing it differently. Add anything else that you have noticed in yourself. Look at other people who seem to do and achieve things and use them as a model. Put this and similar lists into an emergency box (next section).

Section 20

BUILD UP YOUR RESOURCES

A useful practice is to build up a collection of resources which you or others have found beneficial. Once you start looking, you will see that there is a wealth of ideas out there, but here are a couple to get you started:

THE EMERGENCY BOX

Create an 'emergency box' for yourself and put into it anything which you find helpful for lifting your mood, providing comfort, helping you to relax etc. You can look inside it whenever you feel your resources need replenishing.

Only you know what really touches and affirms you, but the kinds of things you might include are:

- Objects that are associated with happy memories.
- Photos of places you have enjoyed going to and people who matter to you.
- Lists of numbers where you might find someone to talk to.
- Things that smell nice.
- Any written reminder of pleasant experiences, such as thank you notes, positive feedback from people.
- Something that feels good to the touch for you to cuddle or stroke.
- Lists of favourite music/jokes.
- Cards with reminders of sayings etc that help you get things in perspective or sum up ways of dealing with problems.
- Reminders of achievements and successes.

COLLECT HELPFUL PHRASES

There are certain sayings or aphorisms that can be helpful, (although I would definitely say that some are nonsense too!) Many of them are central to the philosophy of this book. See if any of these might be useful to keep with you:

- When you are feeling good about yourself, other people become nicer too.
- We get back from life largely what we put into it.
- People treat us the way we treat ourselves, and by treating others the way we'd like to be treated, we model the behaviour we want from others.
- Being happy requires looking for good things: you choose what you see, and you choose what you think.
- If you don't have a dream, you'll never have a dream come true.
- Live in the now: the present moment is the only time you have.
- It is your choice whether you get on with life or stay with the problems of the past.
- Here's how to get whatever you want: do whatever it takes.
- Plant a few seeds and you will end up with a garden full of flowers.
- Aim to feel better than you do at this moment, not to reach for unattainable happiness.
- It's good enough to be good enough.
- "Laugh as much as possible, always laugh. It's the sweetest thing one can do for oneself & one's fellow human beings." -Maya Angelou [6]

NETWORKING

- Build up a list of helpful organisations and their contact details.
- Find local groups and courses where self-development is a feature.
- Look (with caution!) online to see how other people work to improve their wellbeing.
- Use helpful websites to download worksheets etc that may help you to organise your learning and monitoring activities.

Section 21

CHANGE STARTS HERE

Throughout this book, we have focussed on developing your self-awareness. We have explored in some depth a whole range of aspects of your experience, including:

- Roles you play and the qualities you bring to these
- Your values and how these influence your decisions
- Your beliefs and how these affect your choices and responses
- Thinking styles and why helpful patterns of thinking are critical to your sense of wellbeing
- Behaviour and how you interact in relation to other people
- Emotions, how they affect you and how to manage them effectively
- Aspects of physical wellbeing and self-care
- Achieving a healthy balance between all areas of your life

We have considered how you might improve your life by identifying areas for change and making helpful choices, so that you will develop a greater sense of empowerment and autonomy. We have discussed taking responsibility for bringing about these changes in a focussed, proactive way, whether or not you choose to work with specific goals.

Using some of the processes and practices I have suggested, you are now at a point where you can begin moving in a focussed and positive way towards the life you want for yourself. Your heightened awareness will enable you to understand yourself and others better, and to seek experiences which will enhance your happiness and wellbeing.

But remember:

"It is up to YOU to make this happen and there's no better time than now."

GOOD LUCK
creating your best future!

BIBLIOGRAPHY AND RECOMMENDED READING

Bridge G *'The Significance Delusion'* Crown House publishing Wales 2016

Dryden D and Neenan M *'Cognitive Therapy in a nutshell'* SAGE London 2006

Dweck C *'Mindset'* Robinson New York 2017

Fennell M *'Overcoming Low Self-Esteem'* Robinson London 1999

Frazzetto G *'How We Feel'* Transworld London 2014

Gray J *'Beyond Mars and Venus'* Benbella Books, Dallas 2020

Irons C and Beaumont E *'The Compassionate Mind Workbook'* Robinson London 2017

Lindenfield G *'Assert Yourself'* Harper Collins London 2001

Lindenfield G *'Super Confidence'* Harper Collins London 2002

McLeod J and McLeod J *'Personal and Professional Development'* OUP England 2014

Perry P *'How to Stay Sane'* MacMillan London 2012

Powell T *'The Mental Health Handbook'* Speechmark Oxon UK 2003

Sanders P *'First Steps in Counselling'* PCCS books Ross-on-Wye 2021

Sunderland M *'Draw on Your Relationships'* Speechmark Milton Keynes 2008

Van der Kolk B *'The Body Keeps the Score'* Penguin GB 2014

REFERENCES

[1] The Johari Window: A graphic Model for Interpersonal Relations by Jo Luft and Harry Ingham (**1955**)

[2] ABC model: Albert Ellis (1957, 1962) proposed the A-B-C three stage model, to explain how irrational thoughts could lead to depression. This was a precursor of modern CBT therapy.

[3] Genogram: A genogram (pronounced: *jen-uh-gram*) is a graphic representation of a family tree that displays detailed data on relationships between individuals. Unlike a traditional family tree it shows hereditary patterns and psychological factors as well as relationships allowing a therapist and his/her client to identify and understand patterns in the client's family history which may have influenced the client's current state of mind. Genograms were first developed by Monica McGoldrick and Randy Gerson in 1985. There are lots of examples online.

[4] https://www.nhs.uk/live-well/exercise

[5] Antonio Damasio is a prominent neuroscientist and has written several books. His work explores the relationship between the brain and emotions and has shown that emotions play a central role in social cognition and decision-making.

[6] Maya Angelou @DrMayaAngelou – poet, educator, civil rights activist

About the Author

Jenny became a counsellor almost 20 years ago and worked in a range of settings, including schools, adult learning groups and the NHS. She taught counselling up to degree level and undertook specialised training on many subjects including bereavement, relationships and trauma. She worked in private practice for a number of years and was a counselling supervisor.

Jenny says: My special interest is in personal development. From my own experience I know that it is possible to transform the quality of your life through self-exploration, reflection and a positive mind-set. My philosophy is underpinned by a number of ideas about how to live a more fulfilling life, including:

- Getting to know yourself and what matters to you
- Freeing yourself from unhelpful influences from the past and the need to please other people
- Taking responsibility for your own choices and decisions

This book helps you to understand yourself better, exploring your thoughts, behaviour and emotions. It assists you to clarify what, for you, gives meaning to your life, and aims to empower you to make changes which will develop your potential and lead towards greater contentment and fulfilment. At the same time, the book addresses the need to accept with equanimity those things that you can't change and to care for yourself compassionately in difficult times. The text contains factual information about the physical and neurological processes that affect how we experience the world as well as a wide range of self-development exercises.

Jenny has now retired from counselling and lives happily with her husband and cat. She has a number of hobbies including painting, gardening and learning about wine.